Buddhism for Beginners

A Simple and Clear Meditation Guide in 12 Steps To Begin a Path of Enlightenment & True Liberation. Why The Awakening of the Mindfulness Is Decisive For Your Peace.

Emily Write   Robert Peace

The secret of health for both mind and body is not to mourn for the past, nor to worry about the future, but to live the present moment wisely and earnestly.

BUDDHA

TABLE OF CONTENTS

INTRODUCTION

Most people believe that Buddhism is merely another religion which is often advertised by its followers to get more members as a way to have a very larger population that may turn into a good source of funding. Buddhism differs from a lot of the prevailing religion. Moreover, this book is not focused on converting you to the means of Buddhism.

Now, because you read on through this chapter, try and start applying the teachings of Buddhism by taking the first task of opening some effort into how Buddhism teaches its beliefs. This practicing will probably be the first exercise also to ascertain if this technique of earning your life better work along with the current economic situation. Moreover, once you can decide whether to you or otherwise not, you will then be in a position to understand the core concept Buddhism wants you to know and understand definitely.

Buddhism is now among the world's three major religions, the other two being Islam and Christianity.

The religion has assumed several forms throughout the years, but in every form its teachings always attempted to draw inspiration from Buddha's teachings. Buddhist monks and nuns are known as Bhikkhus, and upon Buddha's death, they took over the responsibility of spreading his teachings and philosophies. Bhikkhus, they adhere to a strict code of conduct and this code includes the code of celibacy.

Buddhism has always been a religion that adopted a more flexible approach to its practice. It stays true to its core teachings, but at the same time, encourages its followers to adapt to the various local ideas and conditions around them, all the while never straying far from its main teachings and philosophy. With its vast geographical expansion combined with its tolerant spirit, Buddhism as a religion today encompasses several traditions, practices, and beliefs. For centuries, it has been a powerful and dominant force within Asia, touching on many different aspects, including mythology lore, arts, morals, social institutions and more. Within the last decade, Buddhism has a stronger foothold and presence outside its Asian origins, and its influence is growing quickly in the Western world.

The focus of Buddhism is to achieve enlightenment, and because of that, followers of the religion do not acknowledge a supreme deity or god. Instead, Buddhists focus on achieving wisdom and inner peace to achieve nirvana. Enlightenment can be achieved when followers utilize meditation, wisdom, and morality. Followers of the religion are encouraged to meditate often to help them "awaken" the truth.

Buddhism is a religion that is tolerant and constantly evolving. Certain scholars believe that Buddhism is not so much a religion, but rather a "spiritual tradition" or way of life. Self-denial and self-indulgence must be avoided. Buddhism believes in the concept of karma and reincarnation. Followers are free to worship either at home or at temples. Buddhism does not have a fixed symbol of its own. Over the years, several images have evolved to represent Buddhism and its beliefs. Some of these common images include the lotus flower, the Bodhi tree, the swastika, and the eight-spoked dharma wheel.

CHAPTER 1: THE ORIGIN OF BUDDHISM

Buddhism began in northern India around 500 BC. The Buddhist tradition named after a follower known as the Buddha or the Awakened. He was born in a region of north India, located today in southern Nepal. At the time, it was only a part of the large undifferentiated geographical unit that now refers to the Indian subcontinent.

The Buddha is the image of calm and contemplation. These are the experience of awakening, but the Buddha did not always sit in perfect reflection.

Upon awakening, he rose from his enlightened state and spoke to others on the streets of northern India.

The main events of his life occurred in the so-called central region of the Ganges, which is still the site of Buddhist pilgrimages.

In India itself, two major reform movements did not occur in the Buddhist community too long after the life of the Buddha:

• The Theravada: "The Teaching of the Elderly." These are a consciously conservative tradition. It starts in India and is practiced today in Southeast Asia: Thailand, Burma, and Sri Lanka. Try to reapply the practices of the first Buddhist community during the life of the Buddha.

• The Mahayana: "The big vehicle." It is a reform movement that has radically changed. Mahayana spread in different variants in China, Tibet, Japan, Korea, and Vietnam.

Before these movements grew in India, Buddhism was brought to Sri Lanka, just outside the southern tip of India. Transported by Buddhist missionaries in the 3rd century BC From Sri Lanka, Buddhism then brought to most of Southeast Asia, including Indonesia.

Buddhism moved to a northern part of India in China in the second century of the common era, transported north by monks. Merchants on the trade routes that stretched over the mountains of India, Afghanistan, and then on the great trade routes called "silk "road" that moved through central Asia and the main mercantile centers of northern China.

Here Buddhism encountered a sophisticated and ancient civilization. From China, Buddhism eventually brought to Korea, Japan, and Vietnam. You could put together Korean, Japanese, and Vietnamese Buddhism as expressions of this significant strand of East Asia.

Buddhism was transported across the Himalayas from India to Tibet. Today, the Dalai Lama, who is the head of the Tibetan Buddhist community, is one of the most visible Buddhist leaders and, in my opinion, one of the most active in the world.

Today Buddhism is widespread in much of the rest of the world, including Europe, Australia, and the Americas.

Buddha Can Date to 1800 BC

One of the most important calculations in Indian history was based on the life of a certain Indian emperor named Ashoka, who is considered one of the greatest emperors in world history. He was a Buddhist emperor responsible for spreading Buddhism to distant parts of India and neighboring countries and sending a large number of Buddhist missionaries to these places. He built thousands of Buddhist stupas and built thousands of Buddhist monasteries throughout his empire, stretching from Iran to Bangladesh and Central Asia (Afghanistan) to southern India. A large number of stones and pillars, which existed throughout his kingdom, bore his edicts and proclamations on his subjects, written in Magadhi, Sanskrit, Greek, and Arabic. At first, he was a cruel king, killing a large number of his brothers to ascend to the throne. He inherited a vast empire and tried to expand it by fighting against the neighboring kingdom of Kalinga. He won the battle, but the cruel sight of thousands of mutilated corpses during the war has completely changed his heart.

Several traditional historians are not aware of this controversy. They reject Megasthenes as an unreliable writer and dismiss Indian scriptures as pure mythology. And almost all traditional historians are blissfully unaware of the existence of two Ashokas in Indian history. A handful of Indian historians know of this problem; they suggested that the Ashoka of Buddhist sources belong to the Gupta dynasty and ruled India around 300 BC. However, the Buddhist scriptures speak of Emperor Ashoka as belonging to the Mauryan dynasty, denying the arguments of the few Indian historians trying to get out of the riddle. This was the greatest enigma that has haunted Indian historical calculations for more than a century, almost like a mystery to Sherlock Holmes and Hercules Poirot.

Does this mean that traditional historians are pleased and are not at all perplexed by their calculations? The answer is, surprisingly, no; they are still quite perplexed about the most important things.

Ashoka's rock edicts mention that Ashoka converted to Buddhism because of the remorse he felt for Kalinga's war. However, both Indian and Sri Lankan Buddhist scripts differ from this; these writings do not speak of Kalinga's war! They talk of Ashoka converted from the serene teachings of a certain Buddhist monk who is a novice Samudra/Nyagrodha15.

Why are Buddhist scriptures silent about Kalinga's war?

While the scriptures speak of 84,000 monasteries established by Ashoka, the proclamations are silent about this; they mention no activity related to Ashoka Buddhism. The Buddhist scriptures speak of Ashokan missionary activities in Kashmir, Maharashtra, Sri Lanka, Burma, Thailand, Mysore, Himalaya, western India, and the Greek country. The Scriptures do not speak of officials called Dharma Mahamatras in his kingdom, as the edicts profess. It was desperate to be known as the greatest of all the donors to the faith of the Buddha. The Indian scriptures mention that, at the end of his life, it donated almost everything had to Buddhist monasteries. He wanted to make sure that

Buddhism spread throughout the world. In Bengal, a follower of Mahavira designed a photo showing the Buddha bowing at the feet of Mahavira. It decreed similarly on another occasion, promising gold to those who carried heads of killed non-Buddhists! And Ashoka has done everything to convert people to Buddhism as some legends show. He wanted to turn his brother Veetashoka into Buddhism; to do this, he played a drama. One day invented his ministers to sit Veetashoka on the emperor's throne for a few minutes. Veetashoka told him that the death that hung in his head did not allow him to enjoy spiritual well-being. Ashoka then let him know, "On the off chance that you are absent to joys simply because of fast approaching passing.

The Ashoka of Rockedikte, however, gives an entirely different picture. In one decree, he confesses to the Buddha; but that's it. There is no evidence he has carried out missionary activities. None of his rock dudes mentions anything about the teachings of Buddha. In fact, the Ashoka of Rock Dedication speaks of the equality of all religions! One decree mentions:

The essentials can grow in different ways. Still, all of them have their restraint in the world. It is not without a good reason to praise one's religion or condemn the religion of others. If there is a cause for criticism, it should do mildly, but it is so. For this reason, it is better to have other religions. As a result, one's religion and other religions benefit, while one's religion and other religions are condemned differently, condemning others with the idea "Let me glorify my own religion" only harms one's religion. Between the religions) Good to listen to and respect the teachings of others Mistress of the Gods, King Piyadasi (Ashoka) wishes that all we should teach in the ethical teachings of other religions. To those who are satisfied with their faith, the following should say: The lover of the gods, King Piyadasi (Ashoka), does not appreciate gifts and honors as much as he recognizes that the essence of all religions should grow. And for this purpose, many works - Dhamma Mahamatras, Mahamatras, who are responsible for the women's quarters, officials who are responsible for remote areas, and other such officials. And the fruit of that is that your religion is growing and the Dhamma is also becoming enlightened."

Some established historians could not explain these dichotomies and dismissed the Buddhist scriptures as unreliable. They focus exclusively on the rock arts to get an idea of the Ashokan's personality while relying on the Buddhist scriptures for historical purposes. We can see how selectively they treated the whole Ashokan episode - they dismissed Megasthenes as a liar, rejected the Indian scriptures as pure mythology, shook off other Greek scriptures. They even turned away scriptures from the Buddhists! I think they have a lot to do when it comes to the Ashokan episode, also though they currently think their calculations are perfect.

All the confusion arose because there are two Emperor Ashoka's, and they are both Buddhists! The Ashoka of Buddhist scriptures belong to the Mauryan dynasty of 1500 BC. He was a compulsive man, devout, and took steps to spread his religion far and wide by sending missionaries and buildings. The Buddhist scriptures speak of Ashoka, the Mauritian. The scriptures are mainly about parts of India - Kashmir, Maharashtra, Mysore, Himalayas, West Indies. Buddhism was not widespread in India so the scriptures speak of the spread of Buddhism in India under the Moorish Emperor Ashoka.

The Ashoka of Edicts belongs to the Gupta dynasty of 300 BC. He was the one involved in the Kalinga War. It felt repentant and later converted to Buddhism. In his time, however, Buddhism was already widespread, and he did not have to send missionaries. Also, Buddhism experienced the surge of Sankaracharya in its day, and the Vedic religion made a comeback. As we will see later in this discussion, because of the theological attack of Sankaracharya, Buddhism was in a confused state regarding its ideology. Buddhism was in transition and offered little scope for missionary activity. So, Ashoka, the Gupta was not in a bad mood about his religion, but more tolerant of all faiths. And the places mentioned in its ordinances are mostly its neighboring kingdoms - the directives do not talk about locations within India.

The two Ashoka's are entirely different. If we think that the decrees have a place with one sovereign, while the stupas and religious communities have a home with another, the riddle is comprehended.

Students of history combined the two Ashoka's into one.

So if as per the Buddhist sacred writings, the date is 1500 BC. From the Buddhist Moorish Emperor Ashoka, we can rapidly get to the hour of the Buddha. Buddha goes before Ashoka by 200 and eighteen years. These would Buddha so somewhere close to 1700 BC. Chr. What's more, 1800 v. Chr. These relate roughly to the strict estimations, the Buddha's date to around 1800-1900 v. Chr. Dating.

What is Buddhism?

What is Buddhism? Many consider Buddhism a religion, though some deny it because Buddhism teaches no worship of the gods. They say that Buddhism is a philosophy or merely a way of life. This distinction between religion and philosophy has arisen among Western commentators since a difference between the two in Asia where it originated is not clear. According to some sources, it has around 500 million followers, making it the third-largest religion in the world (if we could call it that).

The name Buddhism derives from the title given by its followers Siddharta Gautama. They called him the Buddha, meaning "the awakened" or "the enlightened one." Siddhartha Gautama lived around 500 BC. In northern India. The exact date of birth is unknown. He was a prince of the Shakya tribe. He is commonly known in the Buddhist world as Shakyamuni, "the sage of the Shakya." These are the only historical facts we have about the Buddha. To learn about his teachings and his life, we must now look at him with Buddhist eyes.

According to tradition, he lived as a prince in the palace until he was 29 years old. His father had overprotected him. He saw no pain or suffering during his life in the castle. At this time in this life, however, he experienced for the first time, the misery of the human condition. He saw a sick person, an older man, and a corpse. He asked his servant about it, and he said that we are all destined to suffer that.

I'm talking about all this because we must understand what questions Buddhism is trying to answer. The Buddha found the origin and solution of human suffering. He said that everything in life causes suffering in one way or another. Then he said this suffering arises because we are attached to things. This attachment comes from our ignorance and deception.

Then he talked about the solution to this suffering. He said that Nirvana is the solution. Nirvana means to blow out. It merely is the extinction of all our desires that causes our lives to continue in a painful cycle. It's hard to think of Nirvana as a favorable destination from a Western perspective, but for Buddhists, it's something very desirable.

So the Buddha tried to end human suffering. He answered no questions about the ultimate source of reality or our connection with the gods but only decided to solve a real problem he had in life. If you look at Buddhism from this perspective, it is difficult to talk about it as a religion. It is more of a philosophy, or even shares aspects with modern psychology.

Mahayana Buddhists have fundamentally changed the beliefs and practices of traditional Buddhism. Some varieties of Mahayana worship heavenly Bodhisattvas and Buddhas. These are beings who have attained enlightenment or are advanced practitioners of the path. They can intervene in this world and save people as if they were gods.

So Buddhism is a very complicated tradition. It could be considered a religion or something else, depending on how we look at it.

What is Buddhism? Who is the founder of Buddhism?

The basic practices of Buddhism are focused on meditation. But the methods of Zen Buddhism go even further.

Rinzai and Soto are two of the seven great Zen Buddhists in Japan, of which Soto is the most common. "Zen" originates from the Sanskrit word for contemplation. Everything can change into "zazen," which is the name of a Zen Buddhist contemplation method. Regular everyday practice is critical.

Buddhists from Monaco invest a great deal of energy pondering, and the part of Rinzai-Zen, mostly, utilizes the reflection on the koan. All professionals of Zen Buddhism look for illumination. Even though the thought is a fundamental piece of the activity, including different systems, it can help accomplish that objective.

Buddhism is religion dependent on the lessons of the Buddha known as the Dharma. The individuals who practice Buddhism are looking for a condition of complete edification known as nirvana.

This religion concentrated on the lessons of Buddha by helping the sangha (meditator) in reflection to prepare the brain, dispense with affliction, and achieve nirvana.

Mahayana Buddhism is practiced mainly in China, Korea, and Japan, and includes elements of mysticism and cosmology. Mahayana Buddhism divided into two variants. Zen Buddhism, which focuses more on internalizing the spiritual journey and self-esteem, and the Pure Land, which teaches devotion to the Buddha Amitabha, are needed to reach nirvana.

Although Mahayana Buddhism heavily influences Tibetan Buddhism or Vajrayana, it forms another major discipline of the Buddhist faith. Also known as Tantric Buddhism, Vajrayana contains both text and writing, including Theraveda Mahayana Buddhism and Buddhist Tantra.

CHAPTER 2: THE TEACHINGS OF BUDDHISM

Dharma – The Path to Perfect Enlightenment

When the Buddha reached Nirvana, he did this by following the path of the dharma. In Buddhism, dharma refers to a sort of cosmic law and order – a way of thinking that believes there is a greater force at work than anything within us; not a divine god, but a divine force that ensures the scales are always balanced. Dharma is one of the 3 jewels of the Buddha, which we discuss later. The dharma can be thought of as the binding beliefs surrounding Buddhism – binding because when the dharma is realized and acknowledged, buddhas are created; the dharma binds the Buddhist community together under the umbrella of shared philosophies.

The dharma encompasses the entire path to perfect enlightenment, from your first moment of curiosity that leads you to explore Buddhism to the final moment when you achieve Nirvana. The Buddha said that the dharma is always here, always around us. The dharma is the foundation of our reality – it is who and what we are, it is the truth of who and what we are. Buddhists want to reach this "true nature," this "true self" that lies within. They do not want to just see it and recognize it; they want to relish in it, to live in it, and to forget any other self they might have been. Buddhists know that what we have no end and no beginning – it is an eternal circle of love. Everyone – even you – can follow the dharma, for this "true self" is within you, it is just on the edge of your consciousness. You only need to tap into it.

The dharma offers protection from all of the negativity around you. Buddhists believe that the problems and suffering we experience in our daily lives stems from ignorance. To eliminate ignorance, you simply have to follow the dharma. Dharma improves your quality of life. It does not focus on external factors, such as wealth and material objects, but rather, it focuses on improving your internal perception of your quality of life. True happiness comes from within, rooted firmly in your inner peace, tranquility, and joy. Buddhism teaches you that inner peace must come first; without it, there will never be peace on the outside. Inner peace is achieved through the spiritual paths of the dharma.

It is easiest to think of the dharma simply as the truth. It is your true self, your true reality, your true perception of life, your true peace, and your true happiness. The dharma teaches you how to grow mentally and intellectually – it is an expansion of your mind and your spiritual self, an expansion that reaches a level of pure bliss and peace – Nirvana. The dharma is much more than just a belief – it is a way of living your life. In fact, Buddha's teachings instructed his students to release all beliefs and speculations that they might hold.

The Buddha never took a stand on other's speculation and beliefs. He did not criticize other beliefs; rather, instead of offering some sort of judgment against other speculations and beliefs, he simply said that doing so:

The Buddha taught the dharma as a way of life, a way to end suffering, as an actual practice that you can incorporate into your everyday life to reach Nirvana. The dharma is a way to live your life. The dharma is the practice of doing no evil and purifying your mind. There are no scriptures to memorize, no commandments to follow. Instead, the dharma focuses on the actions you take in life, the way you conduct yourself in life, and the moral principles by which you should live your life. These actions include things such as not criticizing others, not hurting others, knowing and practicing moderation, understanding solitude and how it opens your mind, and to always pursue a higher and more open state of mind. The dharma not only focuses on how you live your life through moral actions, but also expanding your mind, for without the expansion of your mind to a higher level of spiritual awareness, you will never reach Nirvana, and you will never end your suffering.

The dharma is your path to being indifferent, to being unencumbered, to simplify your life and belongings, to being modest, to being content, to being independent, to being persistent in your actions and goals, and to being completely unburdened. The dharma are the Buddha's teachings, the morals, and actions that he lived by. You, too, can live by the dharma, so you can live this same peaceful, unburdened, untroubled life of simplicity and happiness. The Buddha wanted only for people to live without arguing and fighting amongst each other. He created the dharma as a sort of roadmap for people to follow, a map that leads you to a life free from the worrying, suffering, and problems that plague your life. For with the right perception of the world around you, with an enlightened state of being, the worrying, problems, and suffering no longer matter – you find your peace.

The dharma teaches you that you must first see all of the negativity in your mind before you can let go of the negativity, and live a life of peace and happiness. You have to recognize within yourself and your own mind things such as anger, hate, greed, envy, and arrogance. Once you recognize and acknowledge all of the negativity in your mind, you are free to abandon it. You consciously leave it behind, choosing to know the dharma, to live a life of peace and happiness. Imagine the liberation, the freedom, that you can experience by leaving all of the negativity behind. This includes negative thoughts and feelings, as well as actions. Negativity has an energy all its own – it seeps into your life in all of the cracks, and it takes up residence within your mind. By learning to let go, you will no longer feel the overwhelming pressure of negativity.

The dharma is within all of us; it lies dormant within every mind, body, and soul. It is the path to Nirvana, which the Buddha defined as "the destruction of greed, hatred, and delusion." You see, each individual has the dharma inside of them, it is within their reach; they only have to see it. Each person can let go of the greed, anger, hatred, and delusion within themselves, and they can live a life of peace and harmony. Imagine what kind of world we would live in if ALL people found their dharma, letting go of all of the negativity, and living in peace and happiness? You can, too, know the dharma; it dwells within you, just out of sight and out of reach. All you have to do is see it within your mind and heart, and you will achieve Nirvana.

The Four Noble Truths

The Noble Eightfold Path is one of the primary teachings of the Buddha. The Noble Eightfold Path is visually represented by the Buddhist symbol of the dharma wheel. The dharma wheel is one of the oldest Buddhist symbols. It is believed that the Buddha set the wheel into motion upon the delivery of his first sermon teaching about Buddhism. The wheel is a symbol of the cosmic order of things, which we know is part of the dharma – a cosmic law and order. A wheel is always in motion, always moving; hence, it symbolizes the constant movement of the cosmic order of life.

You will remember that Buddhism is the philosophy of seeking liberation from the suffering of life. The Noble Eightfold Path is a sort of guide to show you how to end the suffering that comes with every life. Almost the entire philosophy of Buddhism draws from this path. Its very essence is found within so many of the Buddha's teachings, so many of his beliefs that he spread to his disciples, and then they spread throughout the world. The 8 practices of the Noble Eightfold Path are as follows:

1. **Right understanding** – understanding the way things really are, understanding the truth of things, knowing that every action has a consequence. This practice teaches you how to truly understand the world around you, a deep understanding that only comes with a pure and developed mind.

2. **Right thought** – knowingly giving up your material home and taking on the life of simplicity, modesty, love, and kindness, extending your thoughts of love and kindness to every living creature. This practice teaches you about releasing the bad while retaining the good. It teaches you to spread the goodness to everyone you come across in life.

3. **Right speech** – never lie, never gossip or slander another in a way that brings hatred and disharmony, never speak ill, rudely, maliciously, or abusively of

another person. This practice teaches you to use kind, gentle, friendly, and useful words, words that have meaning, words that have the truth. If you cannot say something useful, keep a "noble silence."

4.   **Right action** – never kill or injure another, never steal, give up material things, give up illegitimate sexual acts. This practice teaches you to conduct yourself in a moral, peaceful manner, with honor. It also teaches you to lead by example, to show others how to conduct themselves in the same honorable manner.

5.   **Right livelihood** – only have just enough to live, to sustain a living, never work in a trade that harm's another living creature. This practice teaches you how to live with just enough so that you made abandon greed and envy. It also reinforces war and other professions that bring with them evil and harm to others.

6.   **Right effort** – letting go of the negative, embracing the positive, ridding

yourself and others of evil, creating positive, good, and wholesome states of the mind. This practice teaches you to, essentially, let go of the bad while holding on to the good. It also encourages you to show others how to eliminate evil from their lives.

7. **Right mindfulness** – always mindful of the Buddhist teachings, always conscious of your actions, always aware of your feelings, your thoughts, and your ideas. This practice teaches you to always know what is going on within yourself, as well as to give careful thought to your actions. This goes hand-in-hand with letting go of the negativity and embracing the good in life. It teaches you to be always conscious and aware at every moment so that you will always put forth kindness, love, and happiness.

8. **Right concentration** – practice meditation, develop your mindfulness, train and discipline your mind. This practice teaches you the stages of meditation. This

first stage is when you discard all unwholesome thoughts from your mind, feeling only joy. The second stage is when you, essentially, clear your mind of any mental activities, teaching it to become still and tranquil, while you still feel the happiness and joy. The third stage teaches you to let go of the joy while still remaining happy. The fourth stage of meditation is when you release even the feelings of happiness, when your mind is a pure place, feeling and thinking nothing, only being aware.

There is no right or wrong numerical order in which to follow the practices of the Noble Eightfold Path. The list is just that – a list of the practices. The primary goal of a burgeoning Buddhist is to develop each practice at the same time. Each practice builds upon other practices. As a Buddhist, you must work to develop the practices within yourself as far as you are capable of doing. Each practice is going to take time to nurture and develop. Do not expect immediate results – the path of Buddhism is a long one, one that is full of many, many steps.

The Eightfold Path is a path that is followed, practiced, and developed within yourself. Your path is not going to be the same as your fellow Buddhist's path. Each path is individual, each practice developed at your own pace, within your own skills. The Eightfold Path teaches you self-discipline, self-development, and self-purification. It is not a religious path upon which you will participate in a ceremony or a form of prayer or worship. This is the path of the Buddha, the very one that he followed, to reach freedom, peace, and perfect happiness – to reach Nirvana.

The Four Noble Truths are understood and accepted by the Buddhas as the true reality. Buddhist teachings reveal that the Buddha began teaching the Four Noble Truths as soon as he had experienced enlightenment.

According to these truths, all beings crave and cling to things and states that are not permanent. This leads to suffering, which in turn ensnares the beings who are stuck in the never-ending cycle of rebirth, suffering, and dying.

However, a path leads beyond this cycle. It is through the Fourth Noble Truth: The Middle Path. The Buddhas encourage those who wish to be awakened from the cycle, not just to understand, but also experience The Middle Path.

To understand and practice the Middle Path, it is a prerequisite to first gain a deeper understanding of all Four Noble Truths. Emeritus Professor Geoffrey Samuels, who played a crucial role in bringing the teachings of Buddhism to the Western world, explained that the Four Noble Truths reveal what needs to be understood to begin the path that leads to enlightenment.

Here are the Four Noble Truths:

Desire or Suffering (Dukkha)

The First Noble Truth teaches that one's desires are impossible to satisfy, and this causes pain or suffering.

Some liken the Four Noble Truths to be analogous to traditional Indian medicine, with the First Noble Truth, being the diagnosis. In other words, it identifies and seeks to describe the disease in the form of Desire or Suffering. Some see this Noble Truth as a mere acknowledgement of the fact that people do suffer. If it's easier to understand in that way, by all means, adopt this stance while keeping your mind open to other interpretations.

Try the following exercise to consider how the First Noble Truth applies to your own life. Pause and reflect for a while on whether you have ever experienced feeling permanently satisfied. When you come to think of it, the concept of setting and attaining goals often leads to even more aspirations.

We as humans are in a constant cycle of yearning for a satisfying end to everything we do. However, this in itself is impossible to do since achieving one goal, object, relationship, etc., opens doors to the next want. In today's society of excess, it is even more difficult to find yourself satisfied. When we finally reach that financial goal for retirement, we strive to live other experiences that will satisfy us at the moment. Unfortunately, without realizing it, we spend our entire lives searching and wandering, attempting to fulfill a want that cannot be fulfilled. From the food we eat, the jobs we have, the money we make, and even the objects we desire, we are always searching for something we deem as "better."

Of course, while there is nothing negative about striving for your dreams, clinging too much to them leads to the constant feeling of yearning, which in itself is painful.

Since the world that we live in is ever-changing, we need to accept that we are constantly changing too, and sometimes that means moving from one set of emotions to another. You will find that meditation and discipline of the mind in a positive way will help considerably to cut down the suffering, although the First Noble Truth has to be accepted. There is always suffering of one kind or another in the world. This Noble Truth merely confirms that fact and is often shortened to a very easily understandable format: Suffering exists.

Thirst or Craving (Samudaya)

The Second Noble Truth describes the main source of the Desire or Suffering, and it is one's "thirst" or craving for something in this world, which is impermanent. Your thirst or craving creates karma, which then causes a change in you that would only lead to a new desire. Thus, if you want this simply explained, it means that all suffering has a cause.

If you are comparing the Second Noble Truth with a medical diagnosis, you can describe it as the step where you attempt to determine the root cause of the disease or the etiology.

To understand how the Second Noble Truth unfolds in your life, try to recall the last time you experienced pain and then reflect on what exactly caused it. Buddhists accept that when there is a pain, there is always going to be a cause of that pain, no matter whether that is a physical or mental pain. There are always reasons for this pain to happen.

For instance, let us say you remember the feeling of being disappointed about a canceled trip that you had been looking forward to for months. The cause of your suffering is your desire towards the trip. That suffering, in itself, is a manifestation created by your mind depending on what you have taken in over the course of your life. Your disappointment or pain can come from any event in your life that has left you feeling that you were cheated of something.

From this disappointment, you are left with a further desire to correct it. You are then caught back in the cycle where disappointment will surely find you once again. We cling to the positive emotional responses we get, without realizing they are self-satisfaction created by our minds, not our self.

You might think it is just natural to experience this, and, indeed, you are right. This is why it is considered a reality. In a simple format, the Second Noble Truth is that all suffering has a cause.

Cessation of Desire or Suffering (Niroda)

The Third Noble Truth teaches that to end one's Thirst or Craving will lead to the end of Suffering. It is only through this that karma would no longer be created, and therefore one is awakened from the cycle.

Going back to the medical analogy concept, you could compare the Third Noble Truth with determining the cure for the disease, or the prognosis.

The concept by itself seems very straightforward and simple, but the practice of it is what appears to cause us to continue in this self-absorbed cycle. Though you may think that you are kind, generous, and always helping, it is important to realize that self-absorbed is not meant in a selfish standpoint, but in a way where your mind is creating these feelings to entice it to continue forward looking to satisfy your next urge.

So, what does it feel like to end one's Desire and, consequently, Suffering? Naturally, the only way to find out is to experience it yourself. However, the Buddhas often describe it as peace of mind in this life. It's a completeness that leaves no room for want, no space for pride and no disappointment from what does not happen because there are no expectations. Thus, the Third Noble Truth is that suffering ends.

The Middle Path (Magga)

The Fourth Noble Truth explains that the only way to achieve enlightenment is through the discernment and practice of the Noble Eightfold Path or the Middle Path. The symbol of the Middle Path is the dharma wheel (dharma chakra), which has eight spokes that represent each of its elements.

If you go back to compare it with the medical diagnosis, the Fourth Noble Truth represents the part where the physician prescribes the right treatment for the disease that can help you cure it.

Buddhist teachers usually divide the Noble Eightfold Path into three core divisions: Wisdom, Moral virtue, and Meditation. Below is a comprehensive list of how each component of the Noble Eightfold Path fits into each category. You will also gain a deeper understanding of what each of them means:

Wisdom

The first division, Wisdom, is composed of the first two of the Noble Eightfold Path: The Right View and the Right Resolve. By understanding and practicing these two, you will attain the wisdom necessary to attain enlightenment.

1. Right View

The Right View has to do with how you should perceive karma and rebirth. It also encompasses how you should value the Four Noble Truths in mind, body, and words. It incites rebirth and affects the different stages that are being passed through in the cycle of life.

The purpose of the Right View is to make your path clear from muddled thoughts and misunderstandings. Once you have appropriately understood the truths, then you have the Right View. You will likely work with meditation to help you to understand this Right View which will be explained later in the book.

In Buddhism, it is believed that when your body dies, your true self-travels through what is known as the Bardo. The Bardo is a place in each life where you go to choose your next body. It is believed that the closer you are to correct awakening in this life, the clearer your choice will be in the Bardo. If your mind is clouded when you pass, your true self will be lost, making your choice for rebirth often difficult.

Gil Fronsdal, an American Buddhist teacher, explained that Right View could be likened to a concept in Cognitive Psychology. He explains that Right View is how your mind perceives the world, and how this perception affects one's thoughts and actions.

2.Right Resolve

Otherwise referred to as "Right Intention" or "Right Thought," this is where the Buddhist becomes firm with his purpose to renounce living life in a mundane world in favor of a spiritual pilgrimage.

You can take the literal meaning of this and apply it to everything you do from day to day. Having the right intention of actions in every part of your life will help you come closer to that eternal truth. This is an excellent tactic to remember when you leave the sanctity of your home and you are faced with the magnitude of excess in the world around you. Stop and think before making any choices and apply the genuine and right intention to your actions. That right intention is not just about you. It is about the circumstances and everything that is involved in the decisions that you make as well as the consequences.

Moral Virtue

The second division is composed of the third to fifth folds: Right Speech, Right Conduct, and Right Livelihood. Moral Virtue is described by most Buddhist teachers as having the discipline and merit that will lead to karmic, contemplative, social, and psychological congruency. All these are necessary to be able to engage in the final division, Meditation.

Our bodies work in different sectors, and it is important that you are in alignment with not just your mind and body but with the world around you. Remember that with rebirth comes the opportunity to be reborn as any living creature on our planet. Therefore, it should be understood that you are connected to everything natural around you. Just as the roots of the trees unseen underground connect with the soil of the earth, so does your internal self, which is nurtured and lead by the universe.

3.Right Speech

Most Buddhist teachings describe Right Speech as the abstinence of lying, divisive speech, abusive speech, and idle chatter.

To abstain from lying means to avoid speaking anything but the truth, and to hold on to the truth so as to be firm and reliable.

To abstain from divisive speech means to speak only words that contribute to the harmony of things in general. The Buddhist way is to add to the joy experienced by others which cannot be achieved should divisive speech be employed.

To abstain from abusive speech means to use only polite and affectionate words that are pleasing to other beings. Even in dealings with difficult people, we are encouraged to use only positive speech that helps to restore some kind of harmony to whatever the given situation.

To abstain from idle chatter is to use only words that would bring you closer to Enlightenment. You cannot allow idle chatter to stand in the way of the route of your life. Think of speech as stepping stones through life and if you employ idle chatter that is negative, you can think that this is taking you away from the next pebble on your path and back to the confusion of the stream upon which the pebbles are placed.

According to the Buddha, Right Speech is to speak only what is useful and true, depending on the situation and where such words are appropriate.

Otherwise, it would be better to say nothing at all. Silent observation is something that human beings find very hard, though, with practice you will find that it serves more purpose than negative approach and increases your level of understanding.

It is often hard to realize that just because you are dedicated to speaking the truth, doesn't mean that your words should be hurtful to others. Empathy, again, is one of the most important characteristics of someone leading a Buddhist path. Words can be constructive and truthful without being hurtful. It is a delicate balance between each other that we must find. You may wonder if you are justified in being negative toward another person based on what they have said to you. However, it's important to see the positive side of things and refrain from using any language aimed at someone with the intention of hurting that person.

4.Right Conduct

Also called "Right Action," this part of the Eightfold Path is also described in a similar way as Right Speech. Instead of words, however, it is in the form of physical activity. According to Buddhist teachings,

Right Conduct is the abstinence of killing, stealing, and sexual misconduct.

To abstain from killing, one must not take part in the harming and taking away of the life of all sentient beings, whether human or animal.

To abstain from stealing means to avoid taking away anything that is not voluntarily given or offered to you by the being who owns the property. This encompasses all forms of stealing, such as those taken forcibly, stealthily, or through deceit. This is a lesson what one usually learns as a child, although society sometimes blind sights us by making certain practices acceptable, even though they are still deceitful. Thus, Buddhist philosophy covers all areas of deceit, not just those you choose to acknowledge.

To abstain from sexual misconduct refers to becoming sexually involved with anyone who is under the protection of a guardian, of siblings, of parents, of a spouse, of a betrothed, and of anyone who is not married.

Because Buddhism is the path to personal enlightenment, and the separation of those things around you that are put there out of cultural inertia, marriage is not something that is really spoken about. Many Buddhists are married and have children, even some of the most devout yogis, but their relationship is one of truth, eternally. It is often found that those that are married either do so before enlightenment becomes their understanding or after but for more spiritual purposes than current day marriages.

5.Right Livelihood

The Right Livelihood is when you uphold your virtue and to avoid being the cause of suffering of sentient beings. Most Buddhist teachings explain that one should not become involved in the trading of human beings, meat, animals for slaughter, alcoholic drinks, poison, or weapons.

In today's workplace, you may wonder how you can do your job without being in one of these trades, but as long as you are in employment that harms no one and tries to have a job that actually helps mankind in some small way, then you will have begun to understand the message given on this path of the Noble Eightfold Path.

It is believed that anything that is harmful to your physical body also creates a stronger barrier between your mind and yourself. As the barrier becomes thicker, it becomes more difficult to reach that state of enlightenment. The mind is almost like a trick; it doesn't want you to give it up, so things like addiction and culturally learned behavior could be tough to upend. By creating a healthy body without outside negative influence, you are helping your body release the connection with the piece of meat on top of your head, letting yourself take over your consciousness.

Meditation

Another word for meditation is Samadhi, and it is the final division of the Noble Eightfold Path. The whole concept centers in the conditioning of one's mind in order to install discernment into the Three Marks of Existence, let go of unhelpful states and reach Enlightenment. Full knowledge and dedication to practicing the final three of the Noble Eightfold Path – Right Effort, Right Mindfulness, and Right Samadhi – will lead to the fulfillment of these.

6.Right Effort

Buddhist teachings describe Right Effort as your strength of will and mind as you choose to do good each day. It has the self-discipline to choose to think, feel, speak, and do what is good, even when it is challenging at times.

According to most Buddhist teachers, it requires more Right Effort to abstain from ill will and sensual desires. Ill-will includes anger, resentment, and hatred towards all other beings, while sensual desires are all immoral desires experienced through the five senses.

Though certain sexual situations, especially those in a negative light, are considered to be ill-will, sex itself is not discussed much in Buddhism. Your body is your temple, the avenue in which your true self is able to work through to attempt to reach enlightenment. Anything negative should be abstained from.

You may find this hard at first since your mind is accustomed to being distracted. However, when you learn to meditate and can put the right amount of concentration into what you are doing, you will have fulfilled this requirement. The problem that you may find is that you are unable to let go of thoughts which are not relevant to the meditation process. However, everyone is guilty of this when they first try to meditate. If you can simply work your way through dismissing thoughts that are irrelevant, you will be able to increase your effort.

Do not be harsh on yourself for this failing. It takes a while to be able to meditate. Do not expect more from yourself than you are currently capable of doing. As long as you are making the effort, you are working toward understanding what meditation is all about.

7.Right Mindfulness

This part of the Noble Eightfold Path is described as the state in which you become aware and mindful of the present moment. When being mindful of your body, you acknowledge and accept it for what it is. The same goes for one's emotions and thoughts. As you become aware of and acknowledge these states, you let go of worldly desires and all suffering attached to them.

One of the things that many Buddhists practice on a regular basis is extreme mindfulness of thought. When you are stricken with an emotion, especially the negative ones, you want to step back and take a pause. Realize that that emotion is created by your conscious mind and is dependent upon your cultural understanding of the world around you. Then, once you understand the emotion you are feeling, gently remind yourself that it is not the truth. In a simple way to explain it, it does not come from your true self, and therefore it is not real.

Right mindfulness also covers being able to let go of those things that are of the past or perhaps worries that relate to the future. Mindfulness is indeed in this moment. If you look back in this book, you will be reminded of the quotation by the Dalai Lama where he explained mindfulness very eloquently. Mindful people are ever present and it is hard to reach enlightenment unless you have that presence and understand its significance.

8.Right Samadhi (or the state of intense concentration)

The final step in the Noble Eightfold Path, Right Samadhi is about detaching yourself from desires related to the senses and from unwholesome states.

Then, you enter the first level of concentration called the first jhana. On this level, you maintain applied and sustained thinking, which will lead you to experience happiness gained from these detachments as you continue to concentrate.

You will find that your conscious mind is fighting to stay in control. Thoughts and ideas will enter your mind during this stage of meditation. There are several techniques used to clear those thoughts, including mindfulness, which is an understanding of your conscious mind and pushing them out, and breathing techniques. Visualization can play a key role in calming your conscious mind so that you may move on in your meditation.

As you continue to go deeper into the second level of concentration, you experience "oneness of mind" and inner stillness. On this level, you no longer maintain applied and sustained thinking because you only experience pure joy from the state of concentration itself.

As in all other states, this feeling of pure joy eventually fades. This then transitions to the third level of concentration, wherein you become fully aware and in control of your faculties.

The fourth and final level of intense concentration takes place after you have given up your desire and suffering and after emotions such as pure joy or sadness fade away. On this level, only pure and steady mindfulness is experienced.

Many Buddhist scholars advise that those who wish to follow the Noble Eightfold Path should apply all of the divisions simultaneously, instead of in a linear manner. Each of the eight factors is of equal importance and is, in fact, interdependent. However, some scholars believe that the final factor – Right Samadhi – can only be reached if the ones before it has been sufficiently developed.

It is important to listen to your inner self and understand what is working and what is not. The path to enlightenment is not an exact science, it is a path that every person takes and each one, though similarities occur, is created uniquely to your own true self. The difference is that some students of Buddhism who are in their first stages of learning may believe that interpretation is more important than being, whereas the reverse is the truth. It is when you are able to drop the interpretation and simply enjoy the being that you are able to find answers to all of the questions that life poses.

Now that you have reached the end of this chapter, how do you feel about the Four Noble Truths and the Noble Eightfold Path? Do you agree with their teachings?

If you do, then you can embrace the knowledge you have just gained so that you can apply them in your everyday life. The best way to start that is to list them simply so that you are reminded of them in your day to day life. Don't overthink them. Just live your life in a way that respects the Noble Eight Fold Path. When you are able to do that, you will find that your happiness quota improves because of the discipline that you have been able to apply to your life. When

Siddhartha Gautama came up with the Eight Fold Path and it was written for Buddhist followers to live by, it was not in the form of a punishment. It was so that suffering became less prevalent in the lives of people. It works because the improvements that you make to your life are such that they are life-enhancing. Even concentrating for a short time each day on your new approach to life will make life easier for you.

CHAPTER 3: THE DIFFERENT SCHOOL OF BUDDHISM

Buddhism is almost three thousand years old, so it is no longer surprising that it is divided into several schools or doctrinal institutions. These schools fall under two main foundational groups, namely the Theravada and the Mahayana.

Theravada Buddhism literally translates to "The Ancient Teaching," while Mahayana Buddhism literally means "The Great Vehicle." Mahayana Buddhism has two sub-sects, namely the Traditional Mahayana and the Vajrayana, or the "Diamond Vehicle."

Theravada Buddhism

Theravada is the most widespread branch of Buddhism in South Asia and Southeast Asia, especially in Cambodia, Sri Lanka, Myanmar, Thailand and Laos. The Theravadins refers to the teachings of the Buddha based on the Pali Canon, which is the earliest collection of Pali scriptures of the teachings of the Buddha.

Ananda, the personal attendant and cousin of the Buddha, was the one who meditated intensively on the sermons of the Buddha to commit them to memory. Thus, after the Buddha's death, he taught the senior monks to recite and memorize all of the Buddha's forty-five years' worth of sermons.

In 29 BC, the Fourth Buddhist Council in Sri Lanka wrote down all the oral teachings and categorized them into three divisions - the "Basket of Discipline" or the Vinaya Pitaka, which were teachings regarding the traditions of the Sangha, or the monastics; the "Basket of Discourses" or the Sutta Pitaka, which were the sermons of the Buddha and his closest disciples; and the "Basket of Higher Doctrine," which provided the philosophies of the Dharma in detail. Together, these books are called the Tipitaka, or more commonly known in the West as The Pali Canon.

Some say that the Pali Canon is like the Bible of the Buddhists. However, practicing Buddhists themselves do not regard it as gospel and do not treat it as divine truth. Rather, they encourage aspirants to study the teachings, assess for themselves the meanings, and more importantly, apply the teachings in their lives to determine whether they hold the universal truth or not.

Theravada Buddhism teaches the concept of vibhajjavada, or the "teaching of analysis." According to this doctrine, insight should be derived from the experience, practice of knowledge and critical reasoning. Theravadins also place emphasis on the need to listen to the advice of the elders and regard this as of equal importance as one's experience and practice of Buddhism.

Theravada is highly conservative when it comes to practicing Buddhist teachings, particularly among its monastics. Theravada is clearly distinct from other schools in that they believe the arhat, or those who have attained nirvana, are incorruptible. The

Mahayanists, on the other hand, believe they can still regress. Another distinction between Theravada and the other schools is that the Theravadins believe that insight comes suddenly, not gradually.

One important doctrine of Theravada is the Seven Stages of Purification, which they prescribe as the path to follow towards enlightenment. It is believed that every sentient being is fully responsible for his or her enlightenment, actions and karma. They highlight the importance of gaining knowledge through practice and personal realization over belief and faith on what is written in the Pali Canon.

The Seven Stages of Purification, or the Visuddhimagga, is divided into three parts:

The first part consists of the first stage of purification, which is the Purification of Conduct or the sila visuddhi. It describes the rules of discipline, the steps to take on how to find the right temple to practice Buddhism, and how to find the right teacher.

The second part consists of the second stage, Purification of the Mind or the citta visuddhi. It explains the various stages of concentration, particularly the practice of the "Calming of the Mind and Its Formations" or the Samatha.

The third part is made up of stages three through seven, namely the Purification of Overcoming Doubt (or kankha vitarana visuddhi), the Purification of Knowledge and Vision of What is Path and Not Path (or maggamagga nanadassana visuddhi), the Purification of Knowledge and Vision of the Course of Practice (or patipada nanadassana visuddhi), and the Purification by Knowledge and Vision (or nanadassana visuddhi). These describe the Four Noble Truths, the practice of vipassana meditation, and the other concepts of Buddhism, such as the five khandhas and ayatanas. It highlights the various types of knowledge gained once an aspirant practices the teachings.

According to Theravadins, meditation is the most important practice to attain enlightenment. There are two types of Theravada meditations, namely Samatha and Vipassana.

Samatha is literally translated as "to make skillful". It refers to meditation, which enhances one's ability to concentrate, visualize, achieve and calm the mind.

In this type of meditation, the person should meditate on a particular object. In Theravada, there are forty traditional objects, called the kammatthana, where the person should meditate on.

The first ten are the objects that one can directly sense. These are air, water, earth, fire, wind, blue, green, yellow, red, white, enclosed space, and bright light.

The second ten are the objects of repulsion. These include a swollen corpse, discolored, bluish corpse, fissured corpse, rotten or festering corpse, dismembered corpse, gnawed corpse, worm-eaten corpse, bleeding corpse, mangled corpse and a skeleton.

The third ten are the objects of recollections. The first three are the Three Jewels: the Buddha, the Dharma and the Sangha. The second three are the recollections of the virtues, namely: liberality, morality, and the wholesome attributes of Devas. The final four recollections are of the body, peace, breath and death.

Four of the objects are the stations of Brahma, namely unconditional kindness and goodwill, sympathetic joy over another being's success, compassion and equanimity or even-mindedness.

The next four objects are the formless states that are infinite space, infinite nothingness, infinite consciousness, and neither perception nor non-perception.

The next object is the aharepatikulasanna, or the perception of disgust to foods. The last object to meditate on is the group of four elements – the fire, earth, air and water.

By meditating on the kammatthana through Samatha meditation, a person can then enhance his jnana, or skill of the mind. As soon as that happens, he can move on to practicing Vipassana.

Vipassana means "abstract understanding" or "insight". It is the second type of Theravada meditation, which focuses on gaining insight into the real nature of truth or reality. Per Theravadins, nirvana can only be reached if one practices in life the

Noble Eightfold Path, including mindfulness meditation.

In modern Burmese Vipassana, the meditation consists of four stages. In the first stage, the person concentrates on discovering the connection that the body and mind are as one. It is also to see phenomena as impermanent, or appearing and ceasing. In the second stage, the practice of meditation no longer becomes an effort, but one that is purely enjoyed. In the third stage, the feeling of joy in practicing meditation disappears and what remains is happiness.

In the final stage, the person attains pure mindfulness, which will then lead to direct knowledge. It is also in this stage when the person gains insight on the true nature of reality, and it is that all phenomena are impermanent. After gaining this knowledge, the person reaches nirvana, which is the highest goal of all Theravadins.

Mahayana Buddhism

Mahayana, or the "Great Vehicle" was traditionally called the Bodhisattva Yana or the "Bodhisattva Vehicle". It is regarded as the "vehicle" that will bring the Bodhisattva (those seeking to become Buddhas) to nirvana for the benefit of all sentient beings. The foundational teachings of Mahayana are all based on the belief that all sentient beings have the chance at attaining universal liberation.

Many Mahayanists believe in the existence of supernatural bodhisattvas, who are utterly devoted to the perfections, to liberation of all sentient beings, and to the ultimate knowledge.

Unlike Theravadins, the Mahayanists believe that attaining nirvana is not the ultimate goal in Buddhism. Rather, they believe that one should resolve to free all sentient beings and not just the self from samsara. Those who wish to follow this aspiration are the Bodhisattva.

The Bodhisattva intend to achieve this aspiration as quickly as they can so they can benefit an infinite number of sentient beings. High level Bodhisattva who achieved the Six Perfections are described as immensely compassionate beings who possess transcendent wisdom.

An interesting thing to note about Mahayana Buddhism is their cosmology, which consists of different words and Buddha-realms in which the different Buddhas and Bodhisattvas reside. They also teach Buddha Nature, which focuses on describing the sacred nature of the Buddha so that sentient beings may emulate him and become Buddhas themselves.

Historians find it difficult to trace the roots of Mayana, yet it is more widely practiced than Theravada. Mahayana began in India as well, but later it spread across Asia, particularly Bangladesh, Bhutan, China, Indonesia, Japan, Korea, Malaysia, Mongolia, Nepal, Singapore, Taiwan, and Vietnam.

As mentioned, Mahayana has two sub-sects, Traditional Mahayana and Vajrayana. Buddhism teachings practiced under Traditional Mahayana today are the Japanese Zen, Korean Seon, Chan, Pure Land, and Nichiren. The teachings practiced under Vajrayana are the Tibetan, Tiantai, Tendai, and Shingon Buddhism. You can further explore all these on your own, but for now, let us discuss Japanese Zen Buddhism in particular, for it is one of the reasons why many are drawn to Buddhism in the first place.

Traditional Mahayana: Japanese Zen Buddhism

Japanese Zen Buddhism originally came from Chan Buddhism, which was developed during the Tang Dynasty in China. Those who practice Zen focus on developing self-control, the practice of meditation, insight into Buddha Nature, and the practice of this insight in one's life not just to benefit the self but also others. Zen relies more on practice and being taught by a teacher over knowledge of the Buddhist doctrine and sutras.

The practice of meditation is the core of Zen Buddhism. One can do it through meditation of the breath, of the mind, through Koan, and through chanting. Zen meditation or zazen is often done in the lotus sitting position. During meditation of the breath, the person is focuses entirely on the movement of his breath or on the energy found below the navel.

In meditation of the mind, the person needs to acknowledge his stream of thoughts but should not become involved with them. He should simply let these thoughts arise then fade away.

The Zen meditation of Koan is when the Zen practitioner uses a paradoxical riddle called a Koan to provoke enlightenment and test his progress. The Zen teacher will quietly assess the student as he presents understanding of a given koan.

Meditation through chanting is often done in a Zen monastery during a daily liturgy service. Together, the practitioners will chant the different sutras, including the Heart Sutra, chapters from the Lotus Sutra, the Song of the Precious Mirror Samadhi, and so on. Intensive group meditations are also practiced in temples and centers, and most of which last between 30 and 50 minutes.

Now that you have some ideas about the two main schools of Buddhism and the Japanese Zen Buddhism, you may be curious to know which one you should follow. However, what makes Buddhism unique compared to the other religions of the world is that it does not tell you to follow doctrine based on faith. Rather, the Buddha emphasizes on practicing the Noble Eightfold Path then realizing the true nature of reality for himself.

By following the path, you will know for yourself

whether you wish to achieve enlightenment as is aspired by the Theravadins, or go beyond that and teach the path to other sentient beings as well, as defined by the Mahayanists.

CHAPTER 4: THE MOST IMPORTANT ASPECTS OF BUDDHISM

What is a Suffering?

Before we begin to talk about the meaning of Suffering in Buddhism, perhaps it would delight you to read about the Parable of the Poisoned Arrow first. The First Buddha himself told it to the monk Malunkyaputta.

It began when the monk Malunkyaputta was bothered as to why the Buddha remained silent on the Undeclared Questions. Such questions are concerned with the existence of the world in time and space, with personal identity, and with life after death.

Because he cannot accept the Buddha's silence to these questions, he ventured forth to search for the Buddha himself in an attempt to obtain the answers to these questions. On meeting the Buddha, the Buddha told him that he never swore to explain the ultimate metaphysical realities such as those. Then, he shared with Malunkyaputta the Parable of the Poisoned Arrow to explain why such questions are not relevant to his teachings.

The Three Categories of Dukkha

Buddhist teachings reveal the three types of Dukkha:

The first is the Dukkah-dukka or the dukkha of painful experiences. This category comprises of both the mental and physical sufferings associated with birth, aging, illness, and death. It refers to the pain experienced from what does not give pleasure.

The second is the Viparinama-dukka or the dukkha of the transforming nature of all beings. The experience of feeling frustrated because you are not getting what you expected, or desire best describes this category.

The third is the Sankhara-dukkha or the dukkha of conditioned experience. This is characterized by one's "basic insatiability" that is prevalent in all forms of life and all of the existence because all forms of life are ever-changing, never permanent, and without an inner substance or core. In other words, it refers to constant desire in a way that one's satisfactions and expectations can never really be met.

Multiple Buddhist teachings emphasize that life in the mundane world is dukkha. It does not just include birth, aging, illness, and death, but also feelings of grief, pain, worry, and despair. Being separated from one's beloved is dukkha just as much as being associated with one's enemy is. Whenever one does not acquire what one wants, it is dukkha.

The Five Clinging-Aggregates is an important Buddha concept with regard to dukkha as well. These are:

1.Form or Matter (rupa)

The form of any sentient being or object is composed of the four elements: earth, water, fire, and wind

2.Sensation or Feeling (vedana)

This refers to the experience of the senses of a being, which can be enjoyable, unenjoyable, or neutral.

3.Perception (samnjna)

It is the mental and sensory process that notices, acknowledges, and labels. One uses perception to notice the feeling of happiness and anger, the size and color of plants and animals, and so on.

4.Mental Formations (samskara)

These are every single kind of mental imprints and conditioning caused by any object. They also encompass any process that causes one to act on something.

5.Consciousness (vijnana)

This refers to one's awareness of any object and the ability to distinguish its parts and features. Different Buddhist teachings explain Consciousness as:

•Having a knowledge of something, or discernment (according to Nikayas/Agamas).

•A set of interconnected discrete acts of discernment that changes quickly (according to the Abhidhamma).

•The foundation of all experience (according to some Mahayana texts).

In a nutshell, one can safely say that suffering can be found anywhere and everywhere. You experience it whenever you feel attached to anything, be it your thoughts, words, actions, body, mind, loved ones, surroundings, and so on. The only way to be free from it is to follow the advice of the Buddha, and it is to practice the Noble Eightfold Path.

Now that you have gained further insight into the Buddhist concept of Suffering, you might be interested in learning more about Karma.

What is Karma?

Strictly speaking, the meaning of karma refers to any action, intent, and deed by a being. It summarizes the spiritual tenet of cause and effect, wherein the actions and intentions of a being help shape the future of that being.

In a general sense, having good intentions and doing good deeds strengthen good karma and promote the possibility of happiness in the future. On the other hand, having bad intent and doing bad deeds can lead to bad karma and, hence, the possibility of experiencing pain and suffering.

In traditional Buddhism, karma specifically refers to action based on the being's intentions. Such intentions would then determine the being's cycle of rebirth. The word used to describe the "effect" of karma is karmaphala. You can think of karma as the seed and karmaphalaas the fruit of that seed.

Karma as a Process

According to the Buddha, karma is not an all-around determinant, but rather a part of the factors that affect the future, with other factors being circumstantial and in relation to the nature of the being. It moves in a fluid and dynamic way, rather than in a mechanical, linear manner. In fact, not all factors in the present can be attributed to karma.

Be careful not to define karma as "fate" or "foreordination." Karma is not some form of godly judgment imposed on beings that did good or bad things. Rather, it is the natural result of the process.

In other words, doing a good deed would not automatically entitle you to a future of happiness, and vice versa. After all, while certain experiences in your life are due to your actions in the past, how you respond to them is not yet determined. Of course, such responses to circumstances would then lead to their own consequences in the future.

Karma as Energy

All beings constantly change due to karma. For every thought, action, and word being produced, a kind of energy is released in different directions into the universe. These energies have the power to influence and change all other beings, including the being that sends the energy.

The main reason why Buddhists emphasize the value of understanding karma is the fact that your knowledge of it will help you free yourself from samsara. Once you have recognized that every single intention and action you do may have an effect on your future, you become more mindful of your thoughts, words, and deeds. Ultimately, we are the ones in control of our future, but if we continue to be ignorant of our choices, then it would naturally lead to more suffering.

It's a good idea to try to think of all of our actions having karmic value because if you switch over to that philosophy, you start to head in a more positive direction. Your suffering and whether you continue in the endless circle really do depend upon what you learn in this life. Thus, using the idea of the three categories of Dukkha or suffering, you can take notes of which actions you feel you take that need to be changed, in order to limit your suffering.

Another exercise that is valuable is to try and work on the positivity of your energy. This can be worked on in all kinds of environments. Take the example of Janice that was shown earlier, and you can see how you control the energies of others as well as those that you feel. When you come across a situation which tempts you to use negative energy, try to look at it from another stance and think of a way in which you can use positive energy instead. Quite often the karma that lies in our actions comes from the actions taken and the amount of negative energy shared. Thus, it will always work in your favor, to be honest in your dealings with others and to try to raise your energy level above any negative experiences that you may encounter.

As you learn to discipline the mind, you also learn to control the karma that happens in your day to day life and that's huge. That means that you limit your suffering and are able to live with that high energy in a positive way that influences those around you to stay positive regardless of what difficulties they are faced with. The inner voice of calm that is able to control the voice of criticism and anger is one that helps you to become a human being who is able to work within the parameters of karma in a very positive light. That's important but you do need to make sure that your solutions are not so closed minded that they impinge upon the thoughts and energies of others.

What is Reincarnation?

When you think of the word reincarnation, what comes to mind?

Most people would think of it as the idea of dying and then resuming life once more on earth, but this time in a different form. For instance, if you were human in this lifetime, then depending on how good or bad you were, you could be reincarnated into a life of a king or a cockroach.

Unfortunately, such a misunderstanding of reincarnation has caused most people to shun all the other pertinent teachings of the Buddha. This problem may be because many have been misinterpreting many of Buddha's eighty-four thousand parables.

It should be noted that Buddha adopts a teaching style that is appropriate to the abilities of the learner, and during times when the people were accustomed to the simple way of life, he resorted to explaining his teachings in the form of stories. The Buddha had used the concept of being reincarnated into an animal to explain how one's ignorance ensnares one in the cycle of life and death. However, some who did not understand such a metaphor took the meaning literally.

Now, it is important to remember that reincarnation – rebirth – does not literally equate to the physical birth of a being. Experiencing rebirth does not mean that after death your consciousness is transferred to the fetus of a dog.

The True Meaning of Reincarnation

The term "reincarnation" (sometimes called "rebirth" in English books about Buddhism) does not have a direct translation in the languages of Sanskrit and Pali. Instead, traditional Buddhist teachings describe the concept using a variety of terms, but all of which represent the crucial step in the never-ending cycle of samsara. The terms Pali and Sanskrit are also termed samsara which means "wandering about," and it refers to the universal process of being reborn over and over again.

The Ten Realms of Being

Concerning reincarnation in traditional Buddhism, there exist the Ten Realms of Being. Also known as the Ten Spiritual Realms, they represent the ten conditions of life which living beings experience each moment of their lives.

The Ten Realms of Being are comprised of Six Lower Realms of Desire, namely Hell, Hunger, Brutality, Arrogance, Passionate Idealism, and Rapture. The remaining are the Four Higher Realms of Nobility, namely Learning, Absorption, Bodhisattvahood, and Buddhahood. Buddhist modernists usually interpret these ten realms as states of mind instead of viewed in the literal sense.

What is Nirvana?

Nirvana embodies the ultimate aspiration of Buddhists, which is to attain Enlightenment and be free from the cycle of samsara. In Buddhism, Nirvana is the state of the Non-Self (anatta) and of Emptiness (sunyata) because one is free from desire and self-centeredness. Many Buddhist scholars recognize two states of Nirvana, which are the "Nirvana with a

Remainder" (sopadhishesa-nirvana) and the "Final Nirvana" (anupadhishesa-nirvana). The First Buddha is known to have attained both states.

The concept of Nirvana is one of the most fundamental elements within the Buddhist tradition, embodying the ultimate goal of the Buddhist practice. Despite its significance, it is not as cut and dry as the other elements within Buddhism. Shrouded in mystery, Nirvana is the source of endless speculation and even debate, creating significant differences between different schools of Buddhist ideology. While the basic concept of Nirvana is largely agreed upon specific details about its nature remain a matter left to individual belief. In the end, Nirvana is an aspect of Buddhism that serves to find common ground with many non-Buddhist traditions. However, it also serves to find a difference of opinion within the Buddhist community as a whole. In this light, Nirvana is one of the few actual mysteries to be found within the Buddhist tradition.

Perhaps one of the main reasons why Buddhism lacks mystery, in general, is the fact that the Buddha clearly defined the fundamental principles of

Buddhism in his teachings. The Four Noble Truths break down the nature of life and suffering in such a basic way that there is little room for confusion of any sort. The basic idea that craving leads to suffering, and that the Eightfold Path will help a person to eliminate craving, and thus eliminate suffering, is about as simple and straightforward as it gets. The real problem is that the Buddha did not go into as great of detail when describing Nirvana as he did when describing everything else. To make matters even worse, Buddha did not encourage any real contemplation or speculation of Nirvana. Instead, the teachings of the Buddha place complete focus on the here and now and the actions that a person performs at this time.

The whole point of this focus was that by taking care of the here and now a person would arrive at Nirvana in due course. Thinking of Nirvana could actually be a dangerous thing. For one thing, the more time a person spends contemplating Nirvana is the less time they will spend focusing on the moment they are in. Since this is contrary to the basic principles of the Buddhist tradition, it makes sense that Buddha would not encourage such speculation. Additionally, if a person perfects their actions simply for the sake of attaining Nirvana, then a certain self-serving element enters the equation. As long as a person focuses on following the Eightfold Path simply for the sake of the Path itself then their actions are selfless. However, if the goal is to experience Nirvana, then there exists a hope for personal gain. Since personal gain leads to craving, then the idea of pursuing Nirvana becomes a very dangerous one indeed. As a result, Buddha said enough about Nirvana to make it a real aspect of Buddhist tradition, but not so much that it could become a hindrance to the other practices within the tradition.

The Basics of Nirvana

One of the aspects of Nirvana that can be agreed upon by everyone is the meaning of the word itself. Nirvana literally means 'cooling off' or 'blowing out'. While there are some debate and speculation over the precise reason why Buddha chose this word to describe a particular state of being it is generally agreed upon that it refers to the elimination of suffering. The craving and attachment (dukkha) that causes suffering in this life are often described as the fires of suffering. This same sense can be seen in modern terms outside of Buddhist traditions. Such terms as 'heat of passion', or 'fiery ambition' create the same images that the Buddha himself conveyed so many centuries ago. Since the Eightfold Path is the method by which a person can rid themselves of such passions and ambitions, it stands to reason that the end result of a successful journey on the Path would lead to those fires being extinguished. Thus, the terms 'cooling off' or 'blowing out' make perfect sense in the context of eradicating those things which cause suffering.

Another aspect of Nirvana, which almost everyone agrees upon is the sense that it is a destination to move toward. In terms of the Eightfold Path, this makes particularly good sense. After all, of what good is a path if it doesn't lead somewhere? Therefore, envisioning a state of existence that is free of the suffering associated with this life is a very necessary thing for anyone who wants to commit to following the Eightfold Path. Just as a person would be reluctant to drive down a street where they didn't know the outcome, so too, anyone would be hard-pressed to follow a path of life if they weren't at least somewhat sure of where that path would lead. Additionally, the fact that there are two basic paths leading to Nirvana is also largely agreed upon. The first path is that of the Eightfold Path. In this instance a person moves toward Nirvana in a gradual way, getting one step closer with each correct action that they take within the instruction of the Eightfold Path. The second path toward Nirvana is through enlightenment. This path can take a lifetime to achieve, just as the Eightfold Path, or it can happen instantaneously at any given time. Regardless of how or how quickly a person achieves enlightenment the one thing that is sure is that it will bring them to a state of Nirvana, even if only for a moment. And here is where the agreement on Nirvana comes to a virtual end.

Nirvana with a Remainder

According to ancient Buddhist texts, the Nirvana with a Remainder refers to the attainment of nirvana – freedom from samsara – within a single lifetime. This takes place when the Three Fires (Delusion or Confusion, Greed or Sensual Attachment, and Aversion or Ill Will) have been extinguished. However, there is still a "remainder" of the five Clinging-

Aggregates, although this is merely ashes and no longer "burning." Richard Gombrich, a Buddhist scholar, defined the Five Clinging-Aggregates as the firewood that feeds the Three Fires. In order to stop fueling the Three Fires, the aspirant should make the effort to let go of the firewood. By doing so, one can reach the transcendent state which is Nirvana and become free from suffering, desire, and sense of self. Then, what remains is perfect happiness. Enlightened Ones who have attained Nirvana with a Remainder experience pure bliss and have a completely transformed and non-reactive mind that is free from any negative mental states. This is a very difficult concept for human beings to grasp because by making too much effort, you lose the ability to let go and this letting go helps you to grasp what it is that you need in order to reach Nirvana. We have miles to go before this becomes a concept that is clear enough to understand.

Nirvana with a Remainder is almost always the byproduct of enlightenment. It usually occurs without any sort of warning or expectation, just as enlightenment itself occurs. The fact that the Buddha achieved enlightenment after meditating for six years should not be taken for any sense of a normal time frame in which enlightenment is achieved. For a fortunate few, enlightenment can occur in a similarly short period of time, whereas for the vast majority of others it can take an entire lifetime or even longer to attain. No matter how long it takes to achieve enlightenment, it is a sudden and instantaneous experience. Much like turning on a light switch, enlightenment is both that quick and thorough. The state of being that enlightenment brings is a sense not so much of gaining knowledge, but more so of losing ignorance. An individual who experiences enlightenment feels as though they have lost a false sense of self and have been restored to a true sense of self. This ultimate sense of self affects how the individual relates to the rest of the world, and perhaps even the universe as a whole. This all-encompassing state of being is like being in a different world, although still being very much within the physical world as well. And this is the essence of Nirvana—a state of being which brings a person into a higher sense of oneness with all living things.

One of the advantages to Nirvana with a Remainder is that the person who achieves this state is able to share their experience with others. The Buddha himself is perhaps the first example of this phenomenon. After he reached enlightenment, Buddha devoted the remainder of his days to sharing his newfound knowledge with all who would listen. This also resembles the tradition of Jesus in a very real way. In fact, numerous traditions from around the world tell about a person going through a very real transformation and then spending the rest of their time helping others to achieve a transformation of their own. While it would be a large expectation to live up to the example of such great individuals the truth is that anyone who achieves Nirvana with a Remainder can, in fact, have a tremendous impact on the other people in their lives, helping to heal wounds of every type and ultimately guiding others on the path of self-discovery and eventual enlightenment. In this respect, the attainment of Nirvana is as though a person were able to get to Heaven without dying, and in turn, help others to get there as well.

Nirvana without Remainder

After learning about Nirvana with a Remainder, you most likely have an idea of what it means to attain

Nirvana without Remainder. This is the final Nirvana wherein the Enlightened One is "blown out" at the end of his life; there is no fuel remaining. Another way of looking at this is the Buddhist equivalent of Heaven. Just as the Christian concept of Heaven involves a righteous soul attaining a higher state of being after being separated from their physical body through the process of death, so too, Nirvana without Remainder is the notion that the consciousness of the individual is fully released from the sufferings experienced in the physical realm through the process of death. This is the aspect of Nirvana that serves to unite Buddhism with certain non-Buddhist traditions. The idea of an afterlife paints an almost religious face of the Buddhist tradition, making it akin to Christianity, Islam, Judaism and numerous other traditions that hold firmly to a belief in a spiritual afterlife. However, this is also the area that perhaps creates the biggest difference between different schools of the Buddhist tradition.

One of the biggest issues with the idea of Nirvana as a type of afterlife is the aspect of a soul. Many Buddhist traditions don't actually believe in a soul the way that other traditions do. Instead of having a spiritual identity that goes from lifetime to lifetime a person is believed to simply be comprised of pure energy. The identity that forms in the person is the result of experiences encountered within a physical life. In this tradition, the notion of Nirvana is more like a person being 'relieved' of the ego and individual sense of self that necessarily kept them from being one with the divine source of life. Just as a drop of water in a glass ceases to be the ocean, so too, an individual being ceases to be a part of the divine whole. Nirvana is the experience of the individual's energy merging once again with the divine, becoming part of the whole once again, just like the drop of water being put back into the ocean where it can never be found again. True suffering in this tradition is the result of a sense of separateness from all other living things. Craving, attachment and the other sources of suffering are only extensions from the true cause which is a sense of separateness. By being freed from the physical experience of separation from the divine a person is subsequently freed from the fires of desire, craving, ego and the rest.

Another issue regarding Nirvana without Remainder is the aspect of reincarnation. While most other traditions that believe in a heaven of sorts would see this experience as the final destination, certain traditions within Buddhism believe that karma can, in fact, supersede Nirvana without Remainder. This basically means that even though an individual achieves Nirvana they are still expected to balance out any bad karma they may still possess. This bad karma can be from the life the person just lived, or it can be the karma from numerous past lives, still needing to be atoned for. And this is where it gets a bit tricky. If a person doesn't have a soul in the conventional sense, then how can they have karma from past lives? Additionally, if Nirvana is the ultimate freeing of a person from their individual state then how can they retain individual karma? Perhaps this is why the Buddha chose to focus on other aspects of life besides Nirvana. After all, who can truly know the answers to all of these questions?

Nirvana in a Nutshell

Despite the fact that many of these details can seem confusing and even contradictory, the prevailing belief is that a person who achieves Nirvana is not automatically released from their karmic obligations.

Some claim that a person with karma left to be resolved will not achieve the full measure of Nirvana. Rather, they will experience the transcendence and pure joy of it, but they will remain just below full integration with the divine source. Only when they have paid their karmic debt to the full will they be able to achieve total union with the divine source of life once again.

This underscores the true nature of Nirvana. Unlike the Heaven of Christianity or other such afterlife destinations, Nirvana is not seen as an actual location. Instead, Nirvana is seen as a state of being. This is why it can be achieved both before and after death. In the case of Nirvana with a Remainder, it is believed that a person can drift in and out of Nirvana, much the way that a person can go in or out of a room in their house. This is particularly true in the case of those who achieve Nirvana through enlightenment. While the Buddha achieved what could be termed 'enlightenment with a capital E', there are smaller 'doses' of enlightenment which could be termed 'enlightenment with a little e'. In the case of a lesser enlightenment, it stands to reason that the state of Nirvana achieved would potentially be temporary.

Since other areas in that person's life remain in need of perfection, then they would be unable to experience full Nirvana. And since Nirvana is a state of being, then anything less than full Nirvana would necessarily be temporary rather than permanent.

Understanding Nirvana as a state of being can also serve to clear up the other elements that can make Nirvana seem so confusing. In this light, the experience of Nirvana after death can also be temporary. Just as a person achieving Nirvana while still alive may yet have lessons to learn, so too, a person experiencing Nirvana in death may still have lessons to learn or karma to balance. This can reconcile the notion of Nirvana and reincarnation to a reasonable degree of any mindset. Perhaps the best way to think of it is to imagine the Path as a path that is not flat but rather is hilly in nature. To experience a temporary Nirvana, in life or in death, can be seen as a person climbing a hill and seeing Nirvana in the distance. The sight of Nirvana can provide immeasurable excitement and inspiration, necessary things as they descend the hill and begin the next phase of the Path. Once Nirvana is well and truly reached, then there is no path left to travel, thus the person has reached the final goal.

Even then, however, a person can still choose to remain in the cycle of samsara, coming back in physical form to share their knowledge and love with those seeking a release from the suffering of the physical realm. This would explain the existence of such people as the Dalai Lama, who by all counts should have no outstanding karmic debts to be paid or any other lessons to learn that would bar him from total Nirvana. Traditions from all around the world speak of people who are somehow more than human, and this could be proof of such enlightened persons choosing to remain on this plane of existence in order to help humanity to achieve unity with the divine once again. Since Nirvana is not a location these people aren't really giving up as much as it might at first seem. Instead, they may simply be living in a state of full Nirvana even while taking physical form. And this is perhaps the biggest way in which Nirvana differs completely from any tradition of a heaven. Even though this life is seen as the means by which to achieve Nirvana, once Nirvana is achieved this life can still be lived, over and over again even. This is one of the most wonderful ways in which Buddhism is more than just a promise or a belief system. The fact that Nirvana can be achieved in this life, and constantly experienced in this life, means that there is no real distance between the physical and nonphysical realities. Subsequently, there remains one simple question regarding Nirvana. Is Nirvana more than simply the transformation of the individual? When enough people reach full Nirvana, if they remain on Earth could they affect a transformation of physical life as a whole? Can this entire realm experience the same transformation as the individual living in it? It seems the answer to that can only be revealed one person at a time.

What is Yoga?

In the modern world, Yoga has become synonymous with a type of exercise. However, the word itself holds so much more depth than that. The Sanskrit term yoga actually refers to an umbrella of physical, spiritual, and mental disciplines that began in ancient India.

Specifically, Yoga is a Hindu discipline that focuses on the training of the consciousness to attain perfect spiritual insight and tranquility. Practicing yoga involves taking three paths: the first is of actions, the second of knowledge, and the third of devotion.

In Buddhism, Yoga is in the form of meditation techniques that are focused on the improvement of one's mindfulness, discernment, and concentration. Some Buddhist aspirants practice yoga with the aim of attaining peace, tranquility, and even supramundane powers.

The presence of yoga in ancient Buddhist texts is strong, especially since meditation is a crucial part of the Noble Eightfold Path. There are two recognized types of yoga in Buddhism, and these are the bhavana and the dhyana.

Bhavana Yoga

In the Pali Canon, the term used to illustrate yoga is bhavana. The closest English word to bhavana is "development" or "cultivating." However, the former is more detailed as it indicates one's long-term personal and intentional motivation and effort in developing a specific aspect of one's life.

There are five general kinds of bhavana, namely:

1. The Development of Consciousness or Mind (Citta Bhavana),

2. The Development of Body (Kaya Bhavana),

3. The Development of Benevolence or Loving-Kindness (Metta Bhavana),

4. The Development of Understanding or Wisdom (Panna Bhavana), and

5. The Development of Concentration (Samadhi Bhavana).

To practice the Bhavana Yoga, you should choose which particular meditation object on which to concentrate. For instance, to develop one's mind, one must visualize one's present state of consciousness. To develop the body, one must also visualize the body as one meditates.

Bhavana is commonly taught by Yoga gurus to instill loving-kindness. It is also used to help cultivate positive thoughts and habits. Moreover, it is applied to enable the practitioner to visualize life occurrences.

For instance, those who wish to gain more wisdom can regularly meditate on images of them learning daily. This would then lead to a self-fulfilling prophecy, in which the practitioner actually goes out and does what he visualized doing.

Dhyana Yoga

The Sanskrit term dhyana (jhanain Pali) refers to meditation that will lead to the "state of perfect awareness and tranquility." According to some Buddhists texts, the practice of dhyana leads to the discernment of the Four Noble Truths.

In the Pali Canon, eight progressive states of dhyana are described. Four of these states are referred to as the "Meditations of Form" (rupa jhana) and the other four are the "Formless Meditations" (arupajhana).

The Meditations of Form

Each of the four dhyana has its own unique features, which are described below:

•First Dhyana

The "Five Hindrances" are eradicated and replaced with pure bliss. Tender, subtle thoughts remain, but the mind no longer creates unwholesome intentions.

•Second Dhyana

All mental processes cease, including the ability to create wholesome intentions. Only pure bliss remains.

•Third Dhyana

Half of pure bliss dissipates, and what remains is tranquility.

•Fourth Dhyana

Pure bliss dissipates entirely; therefore, the yogi can no longer feel pleasure or pain. Even one's own breath may stop for a moment. In traditional Buddhism, those who attain the fourth dhyana are said to acquire psychic powers.

The Formless Meditations

After attaining the four stages of the Meditations of Form, the yogi transitions to the Formless

Meditations. These are the stages of the formless dhyana:

•Dimension of Infinite Space

Upon reaching this state, the following qualities of the yogi are given much discernment: perception of the dimension of infinite space, contact, perception, singleness of mind, feeling, desire, consciousness, mindfulness, attention, decision, and persistence.

•Dimension of Infinite Consciousness

The same qualities as in the Dimension of Infinite space are discerned by the yogi, but this time, it includes the perception of the dimension of the infinite consciousness.

•Dimension of Nothingness

The same qualities are again discerned, but this time, it includes the perception of the dimension of nothingness.

•Dimension of Neither Perception nor Non-Perception

At this point, none of the qualities is being discerned.

According to ancient Buddhist texts, an aspirant must not simply focus on reaching the higher dhyana. Rather, he is advised to master one dhyana at a time, before he moves on to the one above it. The mastery of a dhyana means you can enter into, stay in, and leave the state out of your own volition (in that there is no effort exerted). The problem that modern man has is that he is taught to make an effort and cannot easily understand that it is letting go of this effort that helps him to reach a state of better understanding. Thus, when mistakes are made during meditation, people have a tendency to self-criticize which is self-defeating. Instead, one needs to learn to continue on the same path, learning from the mistakes made that growth is possible through the mistakes, rather than letting them become a hindrance in the search for happiness.

CHAPTER 5: BUDDHISM IN OUR TIME

The daily ritual starts with waking up a short while before the break of dawn, leaving time to give respect to the Buddha as a teacher to guide your journey. Early morning is convenient as there is usually peace and silence so you can focus on your actions better.

This is carried out by sitting down in a cross-legged, kneeling position or by sitting on a chair if one's physical indisposition makes them unable to keep a straight posture.

Usually, paying respect to the teacher is carried out in front of a small shrine.

A shrine is made up of a wooden stand with three levels. An image or a statue of the Buddha or a mantra written on a piece of paper is placed on the highest level.

On the next level, one can place an image of a Buddhist teacher or guardian figures, while the lowest level is reserved for offerings to the Buddha.

That can be either bowl of water or Buddhist scriptures.

If you're using bowls of water, it's important not to waste the water, i.e. re-use it for watering plants or flowers. After assuming a comfortable position, one can either practice a morning meditation, prayer or chant Buddhist lessons.

A morning meditation is very practical due to the peaceful nature of the time of the day. It can also be very beneficial as one starts the day in a calm manner which can influence how we act during the entire day. According to Tim Ferriss, best-selling author of "Tools of Titans", almost all top performers, billionaires and icons start their morning with a mindfulness routine.

The reason behind chanting is partially historical in nature as the Buddha used to start the day the same way. He chanted lessons he'd learned because chanting is action and, in its nature, more powerful than words.

Morning and evening prayers for loving kindness are done by reciting the Metta Sutta. A sutta is a discourse of the Buddha in Pali, while in Sanskrit is referred to by the term Sutra and means a discourse of the Buddha.

Metta means loving kindness, so this mantra is focused on loving-kindness.

Embracing the Buddhist way

Buddhism as a religion doesn't rely on faith. In fact, there are only two things that are considered dogmatic in Buddhism – karma, and rebirth. Understanding those two realities comes at a later stage in Buddhism, as lifetime of practice is considered necessary to be fully aware of how they function.

The first thing when considering becoming a Buddhist is reading up on Buddhism. You should get familiar with the basic Buddhist teachings that one could relate to, such as:

- The Four Noble Truths

- The Eightfold Path

- Impermanence

- Emptiness

- Compassion

- The Middle Way

- Buddhist practice

Upon reading those, you will encounter the fundamentals of Buddhism and some essential Buddhist terminology. Buddhism is focused on intuitive knowledge which doesn't require belief in the form of blind faith. If the fundamentals of Buddhism suit you, you are free to start practicing Buddhism as you wish.

If something seems true to you, it is likely that it will reflect in your life. Practicing Buddhism can be a little bit daunting in the beginning especially in the western world.

There are tools that one has to utilize. Those are practice, knowledge and the middle way.

Figure 2. Traditional Buddhist monk meditating in silence

If we manage to change our behavior to be more compassionate and act in a more knowledgeable way, we can focus on the things that we can change and stop worrying about those we can't. That is what the middle way is all about.

When one decides to embrace the Buddhist way that is quite a commitment indeed. One can live in accordance with Buddhist teachings up to a point which would make one a non-practicing Buddhist.

In Buddhism, honesty is very important. So, trying to live an honest life is a good starting point. If you can't keep that up, you can live a more "easy" life (without daily practice etc.) but you should be honest about it.

The first step to becoming a Buddhist is taking refuge in the three jewels. The three jewels are represented as the Buddha, the Sangha and the Dharma.

The Buddha means the fully enlightened one, the Sangha is the Buddhist community or anyone that has practiced what the Buddha has taught while the Dharma is the Buddha's teaching.

If we perceive the world as a constant struggle then taking refuge means seeking peace. The first step is finding inner peace. Seek and you shall receive.

Only by being in a state of inner peace, one can bring peace to others. The Buddha had said that only by bringing enlightenment towards other beings, one can truly be enlightened.

Paying homage to the three jewels is a ceremonial and symbolic initiation into Buddhism, which is done by reciting the Ti-Sarana invocation in Pali, the ancient language of the scripture.

By paying homage to the triple gem you also vow to uphold the five precepts. They include not killing any living creature, being honest, refraining from intoxicants and sexual misconduct.

In Buddhism, these are just considered guidelines however because even if you break them, it doesn't mean you can't be a Buddhist anymore. If you repent you can continue to uphold them and continue your practice.

This is best done in the presence of a Buddhist Monk but if one isn't available you can do it by yourself.

It shouldn't be done for simply ceremonial reasons but in a wholesome and willing way. The purpose of this repentance is to bring about a change in your consciousness – to make you more responsible.

.

CHAPTER 6: HOW TO PRACTICE FIVE PRECEPTS OF BUDDHISM

The first set of 5 we will discuss are 5 Precepts. You can think of these precepts as behavior rules. Together, they create a specific system of morality for Buddhists to follow. The 5 Precepts are a code of ethics, in a way, because they contain the basic "rules" you must adhere to if you want to follow the path of the Buddha. Your moral conduct, how you behave alone and around others, says a lot about the kind of person you are. As a Buddhist, your behavior must reflect the beliefs of Buddhism. There are hundreds of specific precepts in Buddhism, but the following 5 major precepts are the ones that are absolutely essential to the core of Buddhism. The 5 precepts are: abstaining from taking a life, abstaining from stealing, abstaining from sexual misconduct/misbehaviors, abstaining from lying, and abstaining from getting intoxicated.

• Taking a life – In Buddhism, to take a life, you are murdering any living being. It also includes the will or desire that you have to take a life. The more effort it takes to take a life, the worse the offense. For example, in Buddhism, it is worse to kill a big animal than a small one. While both go against the precepts, it takes more effort to kill a big animal, so that makes it a worse offense. When it comes to taking the life of a human, that, too, is always wrong. However, as far as how bad the offense is viewed under Buddhist beliefs, this depends on several factors, including the virtuosity of the victim – the more virtuous the victim, the more offensive the crime. Other factors involved in the level of offensiveness include the being, the perception of the being, the thought about the killing, the action of the killing, and the resulting death. There are also 6 ways that the taking of a life is carried out: by your own hands, through instigation, with missiles, by poisoning, through sorcery/magic, and through psychic powers.

• Stealing – This precept is straightforward. You cannot take anything that is not given to you. Therefore, you cannot steal anything. If you take what is not given to you, then you have the will inside of you to steal. The level of blame depends on different factors, just as with taking a life. The value of the stolen property is considered, as is the worthiness of the owner of the stolen property. Other factors involved in the level of blame include another being's property, being aware that the property does not belong to you, thinking of stealing, actually stealing, and the resulting completed theft.

• Sexual misconduct/misbehaviors – This particular precept pertains to your sexual behavior. It is quite specific in its code of conduct. This precept emphasizes the will to misbehave with someone "whom one should not go into," and actually carrying out the transgression through illegal physical contact. Here is where Buddhism might get difficult for some people. A person whom you should not go into refers, first and foremost, to men. Hence, it is safe to say that true Buddhism is not a supporter of homosexuality. There are also 20 different women whom you cannot go into. 10 women fall under a category of protection, such as by their father or another family member, or by their religion. The rest of the women include prostitutes, kept women, women bought with gifts, slave girls, female prisoners of war, and temporary wives. As with the other precepts, the level of offensiveness depends on different factors, including the virtuosity of the person you transgress with. There are four contributing factors for this offense: a person who should not be gone into, the idea of physically connecting with said person, the actions that lead to the offense, and the actual offense of sexual misconduct. The only way you can commit this offense is with your body.

• Lying – This precept refers to giving a false speech. You know that something that is false is not true. A speech is given under the impression that it speaks the truth. False speech is deliberately trying to convince someone that what you speak is the truth when you know that it is untrue. The level of offensiveness depends on the circumstances surrounding the act of the offense. For instance, someone asks you for a cup of sugar, but you only have enough left for yourself, so you lie and say you do not have any sugar. This would be a small offense under Buddhism beliefs and precepts. It is when you lie to convince others that you have seen something that you have not seen – that is serious under Buddhist beliefs and precepts. The factors involved are something that is not true, the idea of lying, making the effort to lie, the action of lying to someone else.

- Intoxication – This Buddhist precept is pretty simple. You have to avoid any intoxicants because they will cloud your mind, and they could cause you to act without thought and awareness. So, you cannot put drugs or alcohol into your body. Not only will this ensure that you always have a sharp, clear mind, ready at a moment's notice to meditate to a higher level, it also ensures that your body is purified of the intoxicants. As a Buddhist, you always need your mind to be pure and clear, so that you can follow the path to enlightenment without getting off course.

CHAPTER 7: THE ESSENCE OF LIFE AND ENLIGHTENMENT

When a human being has satisfied his basic needs – food, water, shelter, security, and so on – he begins to wonder about the purpose of existence or the essence of life. The Buddha himself had reflected on this especially as he may have been a noble whose basic needs were fully satisfied.

After attaining Enlightenment, the Buddha then began sharing his reflections with others. His teachings were then compiled into what is now the Dharma, and its purpose is to help those who are searching for the essence of their own lives and ultimately attain Enlightenment.

Of course, this does not mean everyone should live life in the exact same way. Rather, it means reaching your own unique highest potential in the same way the Buddha did when he attained Enlightenment.

So how do you begin your path towards self-actualization? According to Buddhist teachings, you can find it by helping others, by cultivating the Four Divine Abodes, and by applying the Six Perfections in your life.

Helping Others

Compassion is the humane quality of understanding the suffering of other sentient beings and the inclination towards helping them through it. Buddhism teaches compassion because it enables one to value life in general. The Buddha himself chose to help guide others towards the path of Enlightenment because of compassion.

To find essence in life in this aspect, you may begin taking on a sense of responsibility for other beings, especially those who are in a more difficult position than you are. Perhaps you can volunteer for a local charity organization or use your skills for the welfare of others.

Cultivating the Four Divine Abodes

Meditation is the recommended way to cultivate the Four Divine Abodes, namely:

- Loving-kindness,

- Compassion,

- Sympathetic bliss, and

- Equanimity

To do that, here are the steps that you can take. Keep in mind that you can always adjust this method to suit your preferences based on your experience of it:

1. In a quiet and peaceful place, spend some time reflecting on any one of the Four Divine Abodes.

For instance, if you are going to meditate on Loving-kindness, reflect on how to describe this feeling. Try to embrace this as part of who you are and by meditating on them, you will find that your meditation has real purpose and that you come closer to understanding what enlightenment is.

2.Visualize a person in your life who can easily make you genuinely feel this quality.

If you are meditating on loving-kindness, you might be thinking of a loved one whom you care for with all your heart. Often, these are the people who bring out the best in us. You can see through their actions and their belief in you what it's like to incorporate these qualities into your life.

3.As you invoke the feeling of the quality, let it reverberate from within you to your surroundings.

In the case of loving-kindness, you can visualize not just your loved ones but also other people whom you do not usually care for in real life. Through practice, you could even direct it towards those whom you do not particularly like. The point of this is that you overcome your prejudices and make yourself capable of shutting off prejudice and being able to see beyond it.

4.Continue to extend the feeling of the quality towards all beings in the world. Visualize it pouring from your heart towards them.

You can constantly practice this form of meditation so that the Four Divine Abodes will eventually become more natural to you. Embracing these qualities will then enable you to see the true essence of life. This helps you to become more optimistic. It helps you to increase your mindfulness and your energy levels so that the energy that you give off is positive and helps those people around you to see joy and happiness in their own lives.

Applying the Six Perfections

The Six Perfections (paramita) consisted of the path of the Bodhisattva. It was designed to combine compassion with discernment into the true essence of life. They are:

• Generosity,

• Moral behavior,

• Patience,

•Effort,

•Concentration, and

•Wisdom

Let us take a look at the practical steps you can take to instill the Six Perfections in your life:

Generosity

To be generous means to be open towards helping others without expecting anything in return. There are several ways to become more generous to others, but in traditional Buddhist teachings, there are four ways:

1.To share the teachings of the Buddha

Leading others towards a path that frees them from suffering is a generous thing to do. It enables others to think and act for themselves and to gain the right motivation to living a truly meaningful life. This isn't as hard as you may think it is. When you experience the positivity of your belief in the philosophy of Buddhism, you are able to impart that to others and to share with them the joy that this brings to your life. Each person must choose their own route through life.

You cannot choose it for them. However, you can influence those you care about so that they learn the generosity of spirit that comes from knowing you. Give without expectation of thanks or return. When you do, you feel nearer to the spiritual awakening than you do when you add strings to the things that you give.

2.To protect other beings

Every day, other living beings, humans, and animals alike, have to live through life-threatening conditions. The only way for them to be saved is by the help of those who are in better positions than they are. You can be generous with your time and efforts to help protect them and lead them to a better life. In day to day life, this could mean giving to the poor or being generous with your time when people are sick and in need of company. There are many ways that you can give your protection to others and it's quite possible that you already do this with your family. Extend your protection to people around you who are less well off than you.

3. To inspire and motivate others

One of the best ways you can help others is by motivating them to have the courage to pursue a better life. You can also practice what you teach through meditation and follow the teachings of the Buddha. When others see that you are capable of it, they too might be inspired to do the same. Inspiration does not involve any expectation. You can share what you know and discuss the teachings of Buddhism, but you cannot influence people to follow the way simply because you say so. They need to see your example and to be inspired by it, rather than being expected to follow a way that is not seemingly natural to them.

4. Offering material goods

Living beings need food, shelter, clothing, and other materials to improve their quality of life. Your generosity in the form of such gifts can tremendously benefit them. In fact, this way is easily most associated with the concept of generosity. In the Protestant and Catholic religions, people give alms. These are collections of money that are used for the benefit of the church or of other people. When you have things that you no longer need, there are always those who have less than you. Offering them the things you know will make their lives more comfortable should become a natural way forward for those who believe in Buddhist philosophy.

Moral Behavior

Moral behavior is exercising self-discipline so that you do not cause harm to other beings. The effort placed into choosing the more difficult but morally upright path instead of the easy but wrong one is one of the ways to uphold this Perfection. Another is to cultivate genuine compassion for others through prayer, meditation, and good work.

Through constant practice, moral behavior will become more natural and spontaneous to you.

Patience

The more you practice the teachings of the Buddha, the more naturally patient you will be. Being patient actually protects yourself and others, because it restrains you from allowing feelings such as ill will and anger to transform into destructive actions. As your patience continues to grow, you will notice that such negative feelings become weaker until you can no longer feel them.

To help you develop patience, here are traditional Buddhist practices to try:

1.Acknowledge and Accept Suffering

Life is peppered with positive and negative experiences, making suffering an inevitable part of life. However, by accepting this reality, you develop the patience to go through these negative experiences. Through this, you do not become overwhelmed by feelings of regret, resentment, or anger associated with these events in your life. The acceptance of the Four Noble Truths will help you with this. The very first Noble Truth tells you that suffering is something that happens in life. However, when you strengthen your ability to accept suffering, you are stronger when such an event happens that causes that suffering.

2.Stay calm

Staying calm in spite of frustrating or dangerous events actually leads to good karmic results. At first, it might be a challenge to stay calm when someone is attacking you. However, by taking a step back, you are able to analyze the best steps you can take based on the situation before you react. The more you practice, the easier it will be for you to stay calm and be mindful before you speak and act or even react.

3. Develop patience in pursuit

As you continue to practice the teachings of the Buddha, there will be times when your old habits resurface and tempt you to steer from the path. However, you must remain patient in your efforts even if you do not always see immediate results. To do that, simply draw yourself back by reminding yourself of the teachings that have led you to start your journey in the first place. You will find that meditation and mindfulness will help you with your patience levels. You will be less inclined to make hasty decisions and thus more capable of looking at problems from a global scale, rather than the narrow focus that small-mindedness encourages. Since you are naturally more generous with people, you will find you are naturally more generous with your time and understanding.

Effort

Effort in this sense refers to one's commitment and perseverance in choosing to do what is right. It also means doing things with enthusiasm instead of feeling as if you are abstaining and resisting from something. Some Buddhist teachers even emphasize that effort is the foundation of the other Perfections because, with it, the rest would naturally fall into place.

To practice Effort, you must understand and acknowledge the presence of the three obstacles that impede it. These are defeatism, trivial pursuits, and laziness.

Defeatism is entertaining negative, self-defeating thoughts, such as thinking that you do not have what it takes or letting your fears overcome you. You can overcome this through mantras, or affirmations that remind you that you have the ability to be committed and perseverant if you so try.

Trivial pursuits are the activities that distract you and keep you from achieving your full potential. They serve no meaningful purpose in your life other than to grant you momentary and superficial desires. While there is nothing wrong with relaxing and engaging in them occasionally, you should work against becoming addicted to them.

Laziness is simply choosing not to do something because you do not want to. You can think of it as a merger between the first two obstacles because your negative mindset towards the task causes you to engage in trivial pursuits instead, a common phenomenon known as procrastination.

The only way to get out of it is by having the energy to just do the task right away. Of course, it would be easier to do that if you equip yourself with good physical and mental health and by applying the right strategies, such as starting the morning right.

Concentration

Meditation is the key to improving your concentration, so take the time to practice it each day. Start with simple meditation exercises, such as sitting and breathing meditations. Then, once you become accustomed to them, you can move on to deeper levels, such as those that enable you to reduce physical pain and emotional trauma. To sit and meditate, you can choose to use a seated stance on a cushion on the floor where your legs are bent at the knees and crossed at the ankles. It is hard for people who are new to meditation to take up the more traditional lotus position at first, and this position, provided your back is straight is a good position for meditation. Your hands can be cupped with your palms facing upward and your thumbs touching. If you do use a cushion for meditation, it's a good idea to sway from left to right and back again to ensure that your body is grounded and comfortable before starting on the breathing exercises. When you start to meditate, make sure that you are in a space that is not busy or which is free from distractions.

Close your eyes to help the process. Then breathe in through the nostrils deeply until you feel the air filling the upper gut. Imagine the air going into your body. Many Buddhists use a counting system at first, but later find that they no longer need to use it because their bodies become accustomed to the rhythm of breathing and do not need the count. The ideal count is 8 for the inhalation, and 10 for the exhalation. While meditating, the only thoughts that you should experience are those of this moment and the process of breathing. Detach yourself from the world and your troubles and when thoughts come into your mind, learn to let go because this is not the moment, although don't make a huge deal of it because it is natural for the mind to process thoughts.

You will find that early morning meditation will help your concentration levels during the day and that this, in turn, will help you to have the energy to get through the difficulties that life presents to you. Meditation is a daily event and should be as much a part of your everyday life as breathing.

Wisdom

The highest level of the Perfections, Wisdom is the ability to discern one's own thoughts to choose what is right for the welfare of others and yourself. According to Buddhism, the Perfection of Wisdom means being able to see reality for the way it is and not shrouded by your own judgments.

As always, the best advice to follow so that you can cultivate Wisdom is by following the teachings of the Buddha. However, if you wish to know how to begin, you can start by determining your habitual thought patterns. One important thought habit you should identify is how you would normally view yourself, other beings, and your surroundings. Then, if you notice that your thoughts, words, and actions are being directed by your own misconstrued perceptions, you can do something about it.

Now, you might be wondering how you can find the essence of life and enlightenment through helping others, the Four Divine Abodes, and the Six Perfections. Well, the best way to find out is to go out there and practice them. After that, you can then reflect on answering such questions once again.

Keeping a diary at the end of daily meditation helps you to be able to see your progress. In fact, it serves another purpose too. When you have finished meditation, your heartbeat will be slower than usual and your blood pressure will be reduced. Taking notes in your diary of your progression and thoughts upon what you can do next time you meditate to help the process gives your body the time to transition back to the normal heartbeat and blood pressure before rising to begin your day. Think of it as your record of the progress that you have made with your meditation and concentration practice.

CHAPTER 8: BUDDHISM FOR CHILDREN

Incorporating Buddhism into your child's life does not have to start off as intense as teaching them the path to enlightenment, though there is nothing wrong with that if you do. The teachings of the Buddha's of the past and the present allow you to teach your children empathy, understanding, caring for their bodies, and meditation. With meditation alone, you can help your child learn to calm themselves in a world where there is more stimulation from moment to moment than most brains can take in at one time. Naturally, since their children will have questions and you can expound on the story of the first Buddha in a way for a child to understand.

Think of the Christian religion and how in tune the church attempts to be with their youth. The young people are the vessels that will continue the traditions they have set forth. This is the same in Buddhism, however, instead of keeping a religious idea you are making sure that future generations learn the value of morals and empathy, something our world could use today. Even if your child doesn't subscribe to the idea of reincarnation or enlightenment, teaching them to treat all living creatures with care and love will make their lives, and the lives of others, that much purer in this world. Here are some of the basic lessons you can teach your child that is rooted in the Buddhist tradition.

Empathy

In its simplest form, empathy is the ability for someone to share and understand the feelings of others. To empathize with one's joy or one's pain will help keep those negative emotions of anger, jealousy, and revenge from growing with your child as they become adults. Empathy also springs forth the idea of helping others that may be suffering in a way you are not. Allowing your child to think of others before themselves will help them become active participants in the world around them, and in a positive manner. Empathy is the basis of action in Buddhism and should be practiced and taught to everyone that it can be. Teaching does not necessarily mean through words. Many things in life we learn from watching the actions of others, especially our parents. By showing your child that you yourself give empathy to everyone and everything you come in contact with, those actions will be repeated by your child throughout life. Help a child to stand in the footsteps of another to try to come to grips with problems in life and to see those problems through the eyes of compassion.

Environmental Stewardship

If you look at the planet as part of you, you will find that the need to care for it as you would your own body, becomes a priority. Teaching your children, the connection they have with the world around them will allow them to see the world as an extension of themselves. Once that is understood then the practice of taking care of the earth, and all the living beings on it will become second nature. Introducing your child to nature in its pure form, from hikes and walks in parks, to trips to other areas less populated than where you are, you will open your child to the understanding that the world is a bigger place than just their backyard. They will begin to feel the natural connection to nature that we all inherently possess. Just as Buddha teaches that you should not mistreat your body, as an extension, you should not abuse the world around you, as we are all connected. Watch as the child learns about rebirth by planting something as simple as an acorn and watching it grow. There is much to be learned from the lifecycle of plants and children love these lessons as much as you love giving them.

Karma

Teaching a child about the concept of Karma can be an enlightening experience in itself if done correctly. You don't want to use Karma as a scare tactic for the child but instead, as a realization that your actions in this life will ultimately affect you at some point. It is important that they know no matter how many good things they do, no matter how much empathy they have, negative things will happen but it how they react to those negative life events that will create a karmic ball rolling in this life and the next. Eventually, your child will do positive things based on their inherent want to them, not out of fear of Karma or negative consequences. Remember that even some of the best deeds done can cause negative consequences somewhere in life. Teaching a child to be loving and giving toward others helps them to appreciate the sentiment of giving without expectations. Giving for giving's sake is part of the Buddhist way of life and they can take pleasure in being compassionate and always ready to give even when the only return is the satisfaction of giving.

Intention

So often we live our lives from moment to moment without really thinking about the things we do or the intention behind them. This is itself can create a plethora of negative consequences and Karma, even if it was not what we set out to do. Remembering your intention in every moment will help you and your child make the choices that best assist in a better world, not just a better life. Remember that once a person has to reach Enlightenment their life does not stop. From there, it is their path to have a positive intention for everything and everyone in the world. Without understanding your own intentions, you will never fully reach that state of bliss. As a child, having positive intention can produce amazing results in everything they do. Let your children feel amazed at the beauty and splendor of the world but let them feel the warm glow inside of themselves that comes from unselfishly helping others in their understanding of life's complexity.

CHAPTER 9: CREATING A MEDITATION SPACE IN YOUR HOME

Meditation or Reflection can be a method for changing the psyche. Buddhist reflection practices are systems that empower that will create focus, lucidity, enthusiastic inspiration, plus an unmistakable seeing in the real strategy for things. By connecting which has a specific reflection hone one takes inside examples and propensities for the psyche, and the practice offers a means to develop new, more favorable options for being. With teach and tolerance, these calm and centered perspectives can extend into significantly peaceful and stimulating aspects. Such encounters can use a transformative impact and will prompt another understanding of life.

Throughout the centuries many contemplation hones are produced within the Buddhist custom. Every one of these could be depicted as 'mind-trainings'; they adopt an array of strategies. The establishment of every one too, regardless, will be the development of a quiet and positive perspective.

Learning to meditate

Consistently a large number of individuals learn reflection while using the Triratna Buddhist Community. We show two essential considerations which were initially instructed with the verifiable Buddha. This assistance builds up the characteristics of placidness and enthusiastic positivity: The Mindfulness of Breathing and Loving-Kindness (Metta Bhavana) reflections.

The strategies to contemplation are straightforward. Nonetheless, perusing about them is not a viable alternative to gaining from an established and stable instructor. An educator will contain the capacity to offer direction in how to apply the process and the best way to manage challenges. Maybe first and foremost, an educator can provide the consolation and motivation with their illustration.

Preparing to Reflect/Meditate

When you take a seat to reflect you must create your contemplation pose in a way which is casual yet upright, typically sitting on the pad and a likely lot leg over leg. In case that this can be difficult, you'll be able to sit stooping or else in a very seat. At that point you close the eyes, unwind, and tune into how you are feeling. It is mostly touchy to your experience since this will be the thing that you work within the reflection. It is often a smart considered to reserve some opportunity to sit discreetly before you begin a representation, to back off and unwind. Some delicate extending can likewise offer assistance.

Why is Meditation Important?

When one hears "Buddhism", one with the main things that fly up into individuals' heads will be the possibility of contemplation. While Buddhism can be a great deal more than reflection and consideration isn't unique to Buddhism, meditation is something that holds profound significance in Buddhist lessons. The Buddha himself achieved illumination through thinking and entries that prompt on contemplation practice can be discovered pretty effectively within the Buddhist sacred texts. Numerous Buddhist sanctuaries will likewise on many occasions offer free contemplation classes to individuals of convictions.

To Achieve Enlightenment

For something, how about we cover probably the most understood reason concerning why Buddhists think; to achieve enlightenment.

Buddhism was established not by way of a supernaturally picked prophet or some form of divine divinity, yet by an individual who had understood reality through his very own endeavors and mentally preparing. Not long after Prince Siddhartha, the longer term Buddha, left the royal residence looking for profound freedom, he went over and studied under two in the most regarded contemplation educators in the time; Alara Kalama and UddakaRamaputta. After inside the end meeting his lords, the sovereign pair of on their own experience more.

Sovereign Siddhartha later met a gathering of five monkish lives who rehearsed self-embarrassment. In the wake of attempting it, the ruler at the end with the day chosen to pair off on their own within the wake of finding that this shortcoming of his body from rehearsing self-humiliation made it tough to develop his brain. Following an aggregate of six many years of practice and searching, Prince Siddhartha achieved full illumination since the Buddha at 35 years while thinking within a fig tree in practice he called "the Middle Way".

Be that as it might, this can be recently shallow, reflection isn't critical in Buddhism in light from the fact how the Buddha achieved illumination through contemplation, consideration is imperative as it could be the key for any person to achieve edification. The Buddha didn't merely show that he produced edification; he demonstrated that through reflection, anyone could. Buddhists don't ruminate to "celebrate" the Buddha's acknowledgement of reality, however, to acknowledge it for themselves, firsthand.

The Defilements

Right onto your pathway for illumination isn't the main reason within the matter of why Buddhists ponder or otherwise not developed stable relationships. Buddhists would try ruminating by any stretch in the imagination. Numerous Buddhists think in merely direct sums and considering for 30 minutes approximately a day likely won't enable you to understand a definitive truth about reality at any point inside the near future.

For Buddhists who aren't just as intrigued by complete otherworldly freedom as others could be, you can find to date different motivations to ruminate. Besides the logical advantages of contemplation, reflection is located in Buddhism as one of the primary ways to get the three mental pollutions of ravenousness, contempt and fancy; which in Buddhism, are the primary driver of most anguish. The contaminations exact enduring on us by blurring our psyches and making us stay oddities, by way of example, outrage, begrudge, the dismay of to not get what we need, the disappointment of getting what we do not need for, and so on. Not exclusively perform the contaminations torment the mind with mental anguish, they're the underlying driver of why we perform awful deeds, which in Buddhism, makes negative impacts for all of us at a later date convinced on the Buddhist Law of Karma.

CHAPTER 10: TYPICAL BUDDHIST MEDITATION

Knowing the Mind

When you have a busy life, a full schedule, and little down-time, it becomes easy to get caught up in the everyday life without attempting to grasp a deeper understanding of your life. You need to know what motivates you, you need to be aware of your feelings and your reactions to every situation, and you need to have a clear understanding of the thoughts going through your mind. When you live life just going through the motions and trying to get through the day, your mind is not free, and it is not pure. It is distressed and tangled up in the chaos surrounding you. A chaotic mind will not find peace or clarity – not because it does not want to find peace and clarity, but because the chaotic mind simply cannot calm itself enough to find peace and clarity.

Knowing the mind helps you to pay attention to everything going on inside and outside of your mind and body. This means slowing down, bringing yourself to a mental and physical stillness, and taking time to get to know your mind. Even if you have a hectic mind, even if it is racing all the time, and you just cannot seem to slow it down, stop trying. Instead, focus on actually paying attention to each of those racing thoughts. Do not be critical of your chaotic mind – embrace it, and seek to understand it. The stillness that you need to achieve mindfulness meditation will only come with knowing your own mind. You must know your mind and body to achieve stillness, which is exactly what it sounds like – being still. Not just physically, although meditation of any sort requires that you sit still, but stilling and quieting your mind – bringing your mind to a standstill.

Back to the chaotic mind that is overflowing with thoughts and feelings. Each racing thought – grasp it, examine it, learn why it is there, and discover how it makes you feel, how it contributes to your overall happiness and well-being. When you make a conscious effort to understand your mind, when you take deliberate meditative steps to stilling your body, calming your mind, and learning why you feel a certain way about a certain thing, you are on the path to mindfulness meditation. It can take time to fully know your own mind. But once you do know your mind, you will find that you no longer feel compelled to change anything about it. You understand each thought, each feeling, and each reaction. You will be capable of observing your own mind from an unbiased perspective – and this is a very freeing experience.

To no longer have to battle your own thoughts, to no longer fight with your own mind to be quiet – it truly is the first step in mindfulness meditation. It is liberating because you are no longer bound by the chains of your overactive mind, your racing thoughts, your wide spectrum of emotions. Your mind is free to be still, to be quiet, and to let you be aware of the truths surrounding you. When you are no longer fighting your own mind because you finally understand it, you are free from the anxiety, worry, and stress that led to your chaotic mind in the first place. You are a quiet, peaceful observer who finally understands the reasons behind everything and every feeling – you are someone who knows their own mind, who is in touch with their own mind, and who is at peace with their own mind.

Training the Mind

After you know your own mind, you can begin to train your own mind. The mind is not just one thing that never changes. You are not born with the mind that you will die with. No, the mind is always changing. As we know through Buddhism, everything changes – nothing stays the same. This includes your mind. Think of it as a piece of clay. You are free to teach it whatever you want, free to shape it and mold it however you want. It is your mind, and it is right there, waiting for you to train it. When you come into this world, your mind really is a sponge – a description that is often attributed to toddlers. Your mind is absorbing and learning all of the time. Even as you get older, your mind is still learning every day. As the saying goes, "You learn something new every day." That is so true, especially of the Buddhist mind. A mind without discipline is a chaotic, overthinking, anxiety-filled mind – that is not a mind that is conducive to Buddhism.

The first part in training your mind is accepting responsibility for everything that goes on in your mind, for each thought and for each feeling. These are your thoughts and feelings. While we cannot control another person's actions, we can always control our reactions. So, if there is negativity, anger, hurt, or pain in your mind, it is your choice to feel that way – you are responsible for your own mind. If you do not take responsibility for your mind, you will not be the one shaping it. The outside world will shape it for you until it becomes a mind that no longer belongs to you – it is too affected by outside influences. You must embrace every thought and every feeling that goes through your mind as your own – after all, you put it there. You allowed yourself to think a certain thought or feel a particular feeling. You are in charge of your mind, and you must never relinquish this discipline.

Taking responsibility for your mind never ends. You must always be conscious of your thoughts and feelings, so if you sense them getting out of control, you can consciously reel them back in. To train your mind, start off slow. Teach your mind about kindness. Teach your mind about compassion. These are positive feelings that you can easily spread around you. You have to train your mind to let go of the negativity. You have to give your mind permission to forgive yourself for negativity. No one is perfect – that is the path of enlightenment, to try and reach a level of perfection in thoughts, feelings, and actions. During your Buddhist journey, you are going to have to face some truths within yourself about yourself. Learn to forgive yourself for whatever past action or feeling you had or still have, and train your mind to be kinder and more compassionate – not just to those around you, but also to yourself.

Learning how to meditate, not to mention how to mindfully meditate, is a process. You will not just sit down one day, decide to meditate, and be a professional. You need to ease into full-blown mindfulness meditation by training your mind one aspect at a time. Whether it be stability, concentration, courage, generosity, or kindness, take the time to train your mind in each aspect with due diligence. You want to experience growth of each aspect to its fullest before you train your mind to another. Each aspect that you learn will lead you right into learning another aspect. As your knowledge and understanding grows, so does your mind – you are training it to follow the Buddhist path. As you grow and learn and train your mind, meditation will come easier and easier to you.

Freeing the Mind

Freeing the mind refers to learning to let go. You see, clinging affects each and every person. By clinging, we are talking about hanging onto certain feelings or thoughts – you just cannot seem to stop clinging to them. As long as you are clinging, your heart and mind are not at peace. You must be able to let go of all feelings and objects of importance, whether they be good or bad, in order to experience an awakening, a true understanding – an enlightenment. Some of the things you might find yourself clinging to and struggling to let go of could be pleasure, desire, opinions, judgments, and even material possessions. You cling to what you know, and as a blossoming Buddhist fresh on the path, you are likely to struggle with not clinging to all of these things that have comforted you, kept you company, and been a part of your life for so long. But to be a Buddhist, you have to stop clinging – you have to let go.

Letting go of clinging can be a difficult task for the new Buddhist. You have worked hard to get where you are in life, you have worked hard for all of your belongings. However, understanding that nothing stays the same, and everything always changes, can help you to let go of the clinging. Why cling to material possessions when you cannot take them with you to the next life? Why cling to anger and hatred when it only brings your own positive energy down? Nothing around you will stay the same, so why not just let it all go? Letting go of clinging is actually very liberating – and that is a goal of Buddhism, right? To be liberated. To be delivered from everything you thought you knew, everything you thought was real, and shown the actual truth around you. Let go of clinging because it does nothing for you except prevent you from reaching your Nirvana.

Buddhism teaches you to let go of these things, to stop the clinging, so you can experience a free heart. You want your heart and mind to be liberated, to be delivered from all of the worldly thoughts and feelings and emotions that are holding you back, that are causing you to suffer, even with the happiness. Remember that even the joyful feelings have a connection to suffering because everything changes, and nothing ever stays the same – nothing is permanent. It takes time to free your mind and your heart. It is not going to happen overnight. You should expect to let go of the clinging one step at a time, one feeling at a time, one object at a time. However, once your mind is free, and you are no longer clinging to anything or any feeling or any thought, you will see that your mind is pure, your heart is free, and you are on the path to enlightenment.

Mindfulness meditation is essential to Buddhism because it teaches us how to understand the reality around us, to be aware, and to understand that nothing is permanent. According to the Buddha, we experience suffering because we do not have a full understanding of the true nature of reality. There is not anything in particular that is wrong with you or anyone else – you just lack understanding; you lack enlightenment. That is what Buddhism tries to show you – how to reach Nirvana and be enlightened about the true nature of reality. Mindfulness meditation teaches you to live with a full awareness, to live mindfully, and to concentrate on everything you feel and think, so that you can actually see reality for what it is without any judgment – just awareness and acceptance.

Simple Mindfulness Meditation Technique

Mindfulness meditation is not a form of meditation that you can jump into and be an expert. It takes time to know, train, and free your mind, so that you can reach the level of mindfulness meditation. However, you are likely curious right now about this type of meditation. It sounds very liberating, right? And since liberation is a goal of Buddhism, it seems as if mindfulness meditation is something you should be practicing from the beginning, right? Well, the answer is actually no. You cannot practice mindfulness meditation in its entirety as a newbie Buddhist. As we said, it takes time, lots of time, to reach this level of meditation. However, you can practice basic, simple meditation to help prepare your mind for what is to come.

If you want to give mindfulness meditation a shot, here is an easy technique to try so that you can get a little taste of what this type of meditation is all about. Keep in mind that this is not the whole of mindfulness meditation. Rather, this is a starting point for meditation in general, a starting point that you can use to begin your understanding and practice of mindfulness meditation.

• Find a quiet, comfortable place for meditating. You do not want anything to cause distraction, so comfort is important. Otherwise, you will find your mind straying to your discomfort instead of stilling and calming. Your environment needs to be quiet because you do not want to be distracted by crying children, the sound of the television, or the ringing of your cellphone. You need a peaceful environment to achieve peace of mind.

• Hands should be palm-down on your thighs, and your back should be straight, but again, comfortable. Rest your gaze about six-feet in front of you in a slightly downward direction. You are not focusing on any particular object; rather, you are simply gazing as your mind settles down. If you focus on a particular object, your mind will stay focused on that object. It will not be able to free itself from that object. You need to keep your mind clear of thoughts, so do not focus on anything in your sight – just gaze.

• Focus on your breathing, in particular, the breaths that come out. Stay aware of your environment, but put the focus on breathing out. Feel the air come out of your mouth and nose. Be aware that it is evaporating into the air around you. To get even more focused, pay attention to both breathing in and breathing out. Concentrate only on the breathing, and nothing else. Take notice of the air as it streams into your nose and mouth, filling your lungs. Then, take notice of all of the details as you exhale.

• If you find your mind drifting away from your breathing, remind yourself that you are thinking, and go right back to focusing on your breathing. The purpose of this is to take a conscious note of each thought or feeling that distracts you from your focus, and to put yourself back on the meditative path of concentration. You can even say out loud the word "thinking" or "think" as a sort of jolt to your mind that you lost focus. Think of it as training your mind much like Pavlov trained his dogs – his dogs responded to the bell, and your mind responds to the specific word. It helps to keep your mind clear, to teach you how to keep your mind clear at just the mention of a word.

When you are finished with your meditation session, you should feel calmer and more at peace. Your mind should feel more open, and you will want to take these feelings of peace with you throughout your day. There is no set time that you need to meditate. Meditate for however long you need to keep your focus and to clear your mind. Only when you have reached that calming, peaceful feeling, can you then bring yourself slowing out of meditation. Try not to end your meditation abruptly. Instead, allow yourself to become more conscious of your environment. Let the world around you slowly come back into focus. Darting back into reality can be quite a letdown, especially after a particularly great meditation session. So, take your time in bringing your mind back up to speed.

Mindfulness meditation is a very important part of Buddhism. Without it, you cannot truly practice Buddhism for all it is worth. Meditation takes time and effort to learn, so do not feel discouraged if you struggle to stay focused at first – every minute of focus trains your mind to concentrate, so every meditation session will get easier. Keep your focus simple at first, such as with the exhalation of your breath. As you develop your meditation skills, you can focus on larger aspects of the process. Pretty soon, you will be able to meditate fully for an extended period of time.

CONCLUSION

With the help of this book, you are merely capable to scratch the surface of the items Buddhist practices can offer you. If you wish to learn more about it, then it is recommended for you to enter some from the Buddhist schools that could be near your community. You must be aware though that whatever they will be with instructions on is stricter than everything you already read. It is best then to apply first employing this book, and in case you feel you're ready then you'll be able to begin to take your Buddhist practice towards the next level.

The main obstacle that you could encounter in incorporating Buddhism in your life is your current lifestyle itself. Human beings tend to search for that which was already established. Changing yourself as it follows can only give an undesirable result which could hinder you to see the enlightenment you might be seeking for definitely.

Remember that isn't merely a one-time seven days flick. This technique can drastically change the way you view the world thereby will technically change whom you happen to be for other folks. All you need to remember could be the proven fact that you have to practice that which you learned not as this book told you to do so. This book is merely a guide. It isn't an absolute law that can punish you if you do not abide by it. The author can be a mere human being which is here only to aid. You must then elect to willingly follow since you know deep within your heart it is the right thing to do.

The reward you can achieve will also not result from any power away from reach. All the compensation you may get will occur from you, and you too will realize it soon when you are capable of practice Buddhism inside a long haul.

The difference is that we know it now. Who knows? Only the mind and the mind are simply the present emanations of that transcendent reality to which Buddhism refers, called Nibbana: the immortal, the shapeless, the unborn, the immutable. This is the reality we cannot know directly; the pure awareness called by things like; emptiness, emptiness, sunyata. This pure awareness creates awareness through our mind and our sense organs so we can exist, but this awareness is not part of existence itself; it is a reality. Therefore, we cannot know him directly because we caught in presence, and therefore we are not real. And truth, on the contrary, does not exist.

Finally, people are increasingly asking what they need to do to become Buddhists. It's easy: no baptism, no grades, nothing like that, just a commitment to finding the truth within you. It is among you, and you. You are your teacher. Buddhist precepts are useful, Buddhist teachings are helpful, Buddhist groups and monasteries are helpful, but they are only suggestions for working with yourself. You have to do it; nobody will do it for you. There are no sins or damnations in Buddhism, only karma, which is a universal truth and not just a Buddhist truth. You will be responsible for your actions.

CPSIA information can be obtained
at www.ICGtesting.com
Printed in the USA
LVHW080952060323
741022LV00019B/224